See what marketing professionals are saying about Allyn Kramer and his book:

"Allyn Kramer is the guru of direct mail marketing. Anybody in sales would benefit greatly by adding this book to their library."

> Larry Strong
> Vice President, Sales Director
> Family Service Life

"Covers a lot of ground in a short period of time. Readers will learn a lot."

> Dennis Murphy
> President
> Professional Training Associates

"EXCELLENT! A no-frills presentation of the most cost-effective method for developing bona fide leads ... whatever your product."

> Bob Laughlin
> Vice President, General Agencies
> National Western Life

"Easy to read and will be of great appeal to persons in the lead business."

Gene Grimland
Senior Vice President
United American Insurance

"Allyn Kramer's new book is concise but packed full of useful information. The book will be an invaluable reference tool."

Sharon Chace
Editor
Broker World Magazine

"It's readable, succint and actionable. Great for someone starting out in direct response or for a down-to-earth review of what's important."

David Millheiser
Vice President, Marketing
Lone Star Gas Company

"Worthwhile for people who want to learn how to handle leads."

Leo Arsen
Vice President, Marketing
   Services
Union Bankers Insurance

How To
Master The Art Of
LEAD
GENERATION

70 RULES AND STRATEGIES
To Generate
Pre-Qualified
Sales Leads
Using
Direct Response Marketing

Allyn Kramer

Printed in the United States of America

ISBN 0-9634221-0-3 (U.S.A.)

First printing — 1991
Second printing — 1992
Third printing — 1993
Fourth printing — 1995
Fifth printing — 1996

Prestonwood
Press

About the Author

Allyn Kramer is a veteran of more than 20 years in the direct marketing business. In that time he's become nationally recognized as an expert in consumer and business prospect lists, as well as developing lead generation programs.

Mr. Kramer is a popular public speaker at conventions and seminars nation-wide on the topics contained in this book. He is a graduate of Drake University, holds an MBA, and has taught college courses on direct marketing.

His numerous articles have appeared in trade publications in the fields of insurance, financial services, health care, and real estate. And he is the author of *Mature Money: How to Sell Financial Services to the Affluent 50+ Market.*

As president of Kramer Lead Marketing Group, Allyn Kramer specializes in providing prospect lists and complete direct mail programs to generate pre-qualified sales leads. You can reach him at:

Kramer Lead Marketing Group
11884 Greenville Avenue, Suite 106
Dallas, Texas 75243
972-644-6000
800-447-0533

Acknowledgments

This book is, in great measure, due to the tremendous talent of Michael Lovas. His wonderful editing skills and devotion to this project brought years of ideas and experiences into focus.

Thank you goes to the thousands of clients who have allowed me to provide them with prospect lists and complete direct mail programs over the years. This book is a reflection of the experiences they have provided.

Dedication

This book is dedicated to my family: Susan, Alex, and Andrea, who give me purpose for everything.

Table of Contents

Page

Introduction   13

Part I: PRE-QUALIFIED LEADS
How To Attract the People Who
Want To Buy Your Product

1.	Why Lead Generation Is Important To You	16
2.	Exactly What Is A Pre-Qualified Lead?	18
3.	The New Face of Prospecting	20
4.	How To Get Leads	22
5.	Why Direct Response Works Better Than Traditional Marketing	26
6.	Using Direct Mail To Promote Your Products and Service	29
7.	What To Tell Your Leads To Pre-Qualify Them	32

Part II: YOUR MARKET
Changing Names To Prospects

8.	Where Do You Get Prospects?	35
9.	How To Pick Lists That Work	38
10.	Saving Money On Your Mailing	43

Part III: YOUR OFFER
What To Say and How To Say It

11.	The Offer	49
12.	The Magic Words	56
13.	Freebies — Increasing Response	59
14.	Benefits and Features	65
15.	Holding Attention	70
16.	Humor — So You Think You're Funny	74
17.	How To Put Action In Your Offer	78
18.	Two Faces of Positioning	82
19.	Hot Spots — The First Places Your Prospects Will Look	85
20.	Headlines — Making Them Work For You	88

Part IV: THE PACKAGE
Your Direct Mail Workhorse

21.	The Look of Your Mailer — Its Visual Personality	94
22.	Response Device — Mail Me In	99
23.	Follow-Up Letters	104
24.	Working With An Ad Agency	106

Part V: TELEMARKETING
The Fastest Way To Reach
Pre-Qualified Prospects

25.	Say Hello To Prospects	110
26.	The Conversation — What To Say and How To Say It	112
27.	Credibility — What Not To Do	114
28.	Forbidden Phrases	116

Part VI: DATABASE MARKETING
Creating A Greater Competitive Advantage

29.	What Is A DataBase?	119
30.	DataBase Information	121
31.	How To Set Up and Use A DataBase	124

Part VII: LEAD MANAGEMENT
Controlling For Success

32.	Testing	127
33.	Balancing the Flow of Leads	129
34.	When and Where To Mail	131
35.	Inquiry Fulfillment	133

Part VIII: LEAD GENERATION
BUSINESS STRATEGIES
Ideas For Building a Better Business

36.	Six Hard Knocks Strategies	136
	Persistence	
	List Deliverability	
	Testing	
	Action	
	Client Information	
	Prepare for Success	
37.	Does Lead Generation Pay?	140

Conclusion	142
Listing of Rules	143
Glossary of Additional Terms	153
Index	156

Introduction

The sole purpose of this book is to teach business people how to increase sales and profits with the most logical way presented to us in the 1990's — by using direct response marketing techniques to generate pre-qualified leads.

Few marketers and even fewer authors understand the difference between mail order and generating pre-qualified sales leads. There is a big distinction between getting a check back in the mail versus getting an inquiry from someone who must talk to you before the sale is complete.

To successfully compete in business today you need more than the tools of your trade. You need a working knowledge of how to get new sales leads, and how to screen and qualify those leads so you don't waste time and money.

Besides possessing professional expertise, competitive service or products, and an excellent organization, you need mastery of direct response marketing. In the 1990's economy, you can't be only an expert in your industry . . . or only a sales promotion professional. You need to be skilled at both.

The techniques you'll find here are **not** theory or conjecture. They are ideas observed and proven in over ten-million mailings for more than 1,000 different clients over the last five years.

The rules and strategies you're about to learn have helped other business people become more successful and have also helped to build my own business from a brand new start-up to a respected national firm. Take these tools and use them to make more sales, more profit, now!

Allyn Kramer

"No! I can't be bothered to see any crazy salesman— we've got a battle to fight!"

Part I

PRE-QUALIFIED LEADS

How To Attract the People Who Want To Buy Your Product

1. Why Lead Generation Is Important To You
2. Exactly What Is a Pre-Qualified Lead?
3. The New Face of Prospecting
4. How To Get Leads
5. Why Direct Response Works Better Than Traditional Marketing
6. Using Direct Mail To Promote Your Products and Service
7. What To Tell Your Leads To Pre-Qualify Them

Chapter 1

WHY LEAD GENERATION IS IMPORTANT TO YOU

KEY TERMS:

Acquisition Cost
Pre-Qualified Lead Generation

Because of increasing expenses and stiffer competition in virtually all industries, marketers are feeling the pinch to get new clients, keep old clients, and "come in under budget."

Add to this McGraw-Hill's claim that an in-person commercial sales call requires more than five visits and costs more than $250. You can immediately see that there's got to be a better way. There is! It's called "lead generation" and there's a lot more to it than just chasing names.

I used to work for a company that didn't do any specific lead generation for its sales people at all. Sure, they ran a few space ads, but nothing to get lots of really qualified buyers. After starving for a year, I decided I could do at least as well on my own.

The first thing I did was to start a direct response lead generation program. We became profitable in the second month of operation and never looked back until the company was sold three years later — when we were grossing millions of dollars!

Lead generation works to save you time and money. You move deeper into your market to find exactly those people who are most likely to buy your product.

It happens all the time. You come across a potential prospect which you follow-up and pursue. Eventually a client is added to the books — at an **acquisition cost** so high that your profit margin is minimal or nonexistent.

What is your alternative? How could you have avoided spending so much time and money to gain a client? Better still, how can you intelligently acquire new clients and consistently "come in under budget"?

The solution is to take a giant step beyond lead generation. The biggest secret to successful business right now and in the future is **Pre-Qualified Lead Generation** . . . *the art of getting future clients to contact you and tell you they are interested!*

Chapter 2

EXACTLY WHAT IS A PRE-QUALIFIED LEAD?

KEY TERMS:

Names
Prospects
Pre-Qualified Leads

More than 55% of current sales professionals have no idea how to sell! That is the claim of Jeanne and Herbert Greenberg in their book, *What It Takes to Succeed in Sales: Selecting and Retaining Top Producers.*

■ **RULE 1:** The best way to get new sales people started is to get them in front of pre-qualified leads.

Names. A name with no interest in your product is just a name. Open your phone book to almost any page. Close your eyes and point to a name. That's not a lead — it's a name.

Prospects. A referral from a friend or a name from a list of people who might have an interest in your product is a prospect. Some indication that the name might logically be interested in your offer can turn a name into a prospect. Friendly referrals, directories of organizations, entries for a give-away and names of businesses from the Yellow Pages are all prospects.

Pre-Qualified Leads. People who have asked for more information about your product are pre-qualified leads. Some people mistakenly call them prospects. They want to know more about your product. They are the best leads.

Your job is to convert names into prospects — and prospects into pre-qualified leads. To do this, your best tools to use are direct mail or telemarketing or both.

Chapter 3

THE NEW FACE OF PROSPECTING

KEY TERMS:

Prospecting
Cold Call
Tracking

Prospecting is the lifeblood for generating new business. However, prospecting in the 1990's is different. Understanding how it works can make it work much better for you!

For generations sales people canvassed neighborhoods, knocked on doors and tried to make sales, or at least set up prospective future sales. This became known as **prospecting**.

Today, some people still thrive on the challenge of a **cold call**. Others get weak in the knees at just the thought of picking up a phone or knocking on a stranger's door. Whether you're aggressive or not, you can benefit from the new face of prospecting.

What's new about **prospecting**? Applying direct response marketing techniques to prospecting is new. This means you don't have to knock on strange doors and, as a result, you make more sales, more profit, faster. Like a general in combat, you can sit back, observe, analyze results, and redirect your efforts accordingly.

Yesterday's direct marketing was based on door-to-door sales, typified by the Kirby Vacuum Cleaner or Fuller Brush salesmen. It was time-consuming and expensive. Today's direct marketing offers you a much more scientific and efficient way to make sales and cut costs. It consists of cost-effective, logical techniques that take practically all of the guesswork out of your prospecting.

Because it is a way to reach a large number of prospects in a short period of time, today's direct response marketing gives you advantages you may never before have realized!

Responses and results come to you quickly. Direct response marketing also allows **tracking** (to specifically identify where the responses come from), so you can measure and gauge your success. Then you can adjust and improve your promotions based on scientific evidence, not intuition or chance!

Chapter 4

HOW TO GET LEADS

KEY TERMS:

Target Marketing
Demographics
Psychographics
Synchrographics

Names are relatively easy to get. Prospects are a little harder to get and pre-qualified leads are the hardest to get. Attracting pre-qualified leads has evolved into a huge industry. But the concept is simple. Just look:

■ **RULE 2: Target marketing** to generate pre-qualified leads begins with two basic steps: 1) determine what specific product or service you want to promote; and 2) decide who is your most likely prospect.

■ **RULE 3:** Construct a customer profile of the type of person most likely to buy each of your products. Paint a word picture of that person.

> *PROBLEM*: Let's say you sell annuities directly to the public. You want to increase your customer base with the least amount of time and expense. An investment of $10,000 is required in the annuities you want to promote. The annuities in turn will provide your clients a very safe investment yielding a moderate, tax-deferred interest rate on their money.

First, you match the low risk, tax deferred character of your annuity with the specific personality type that would most likely buy it. To do this effectively, you investigate the demographics of your potential market.

■ **RULE 4: Demographics** tell you if the market you've targeted is able to buy your product. Demographics give you quantitative information about prospects. These are the social and economic characteristics of your market, such as where they live, how much income they earn and how old they are.

■ **RULE 5: Psychographics** tell you if your market wants to buy your product. They give you qualitative information about prospects. These are the lifestyle and behavioral characteristics of your market, such as how they buy and why they buy. Psychographics indicate activities and interests. This information is very powerful, but usually more difficult to obtain.

■ **RULE 6: Synchrographics** tell you when the market is ready to buy your product. They give you the time when something is going to affect your market such as a birth, marriage, sale of a house or business, or retirement.

> After research, you conclude that the person who would most likely buy your annuity is a high-income pre-retiree. You determine that someone between the ages of 50 and 64 with over $35,000 annual income is a prime prospect. They're earning a higher income than they ever have before because of seniority or having gone up the corporate ladder. But at the same time, many of life's major expenses have gone away, such as college tuition for kids, or mortgages that are paid off or are moderate by today's standards.

> These circumstances provide the discretionary income that prospects need to buy your annuity now. And their age means they are approaching retirement and a fixed income which perfectly fits the low risk condition of your investment.

> *SOLUTION*: You decide to generate a list of prospects for a direct mail promotion using the profile you've put together. Specifically, you decide to test the market by renting a list of 50 to 64 year-olds, with an estimated wealth rating of $35,000+, in the three zip codes of your market area. This represents a straight-forward list available from companies that compile names of individuals by age, income, and zip code. And it weeds out names that don't fit your target prospect.

■ **RULE 7:** Targeting a group that is knowledgeable about your product category costs less time and money than marketing to a group you have to educate.

EXAMPLE: If you tried to sell a piece of property to commercial real estate developers, you would spend little time explaining the benefits. You would focus almost exclusively on details such as financing.

On the other hand, if you were marketing the same property to a school board for a potential school site, you would have to educate a diverse group of people on the basics of real estate and how your parcel would be in their best interest.

Chapter 5

WHY DIRECT RESPONSE WORKS BETTER THAN TRADITIONAL MARKETING

KEY TERMS:

Generic
Call-to-Action

Using traditional marketing avenues such as newspapers, magazines, radio, or television means

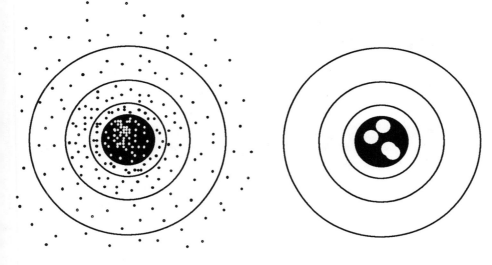

Traditional marketing.   Direct marketing.

using a shotgun approach. Using targeted or direct marketing means using a high-powered tool with pin-point accuracy.

Traditional marketing means talking to huge groups of people rather than to one individual person as you do in direct marketing. Because traditional marketing is intended for a mass audience — often hundreds of thousands of people — the message must be general enough to be understood by all.

Since such a wide audience has little in common, your message must be **generic**. The language and examples you use must be common to everyone.

Another way to look at a traditional marketing message is that it is not personalized for a select audience. You are a tougher competitor in today's business environment with targeted direct response marketing than with traditional marketing to the masses.

If a sales person were to deliver a general message to you, you'd probably say, "Stop beating around the bush and get to the point!" Speaking to widely different types of people results in a watered-down version of what you would have said if you'd been talking one-to-one with a person interested in your product. With a generic message, your promotion is left with little punch and no compelling **call-to-action** (reason to respond).

Chapter 6

USING DIRECT MAIL TO PROMOTE YOUR PRODUCTS AND SERVICE

KEY TERMS:

Reply Card
Response Rate
Offer
Package

Direct mail marketing is an easy way to reach a large number of selected prospects. It's simply

more persuasive and action-oriented than traditional awareness advertising.

Direct mail has surpassed newspapers to become the biggest marketing medium, with 26% of total advertising dollars spent, according to a study done by the Printing Industries of America. It gives you a way to achieve a one-on-one relationship with your prospects without incurring the expense of going from door to door. And it generates inquiries that can be followed-up with more mail, a phone call, or an in-person visit.

Benefits of Direct Mail:

Personal. You can address your leads by name, such as "Dear Mr. Smith". You can even refer to personal information about them, like "as owner of your own business," showing you've made a special effort to seek them out and that they're not just a number to you.

Less waste. You can reach out to precisely the prospects with the highest potential interest in buying from you. Avoiding the mass coverage of newspapers and television saves you untold advertising dollars.

Less competition. Your promotion is neither lost among the dozens of other ads in a magazine nor is it lost immediately in the fleeting moment of a radio commercial.

Measurable response. Unlike general awareness advertising, which is almost impossible to measure, direct marketing allows you to measure and analyze responses. By printing project numbers on your **reply card** you can accurately track the response to each promotion. This not only allows you to tell what promotion works and what doesn't but also allows you to improve your marketing efforts each time you mail.

Statistically projectable. After you mail a promotion, you can expect future mailings to have a similar **response rate** if future criteria are similar. If you mail the same promotion (**offer** and **package**) to a similar list (same characteristics) at the same time of year, you should know approximately how many responses to expect before your first mail piece goes to the post office.

Immediate. You can create and fulfill a desire for information all at one time. Do this by pointing out a need your readers have, telling them how you can help them fill that need and then giving them a way to respond — by sending back the **reply card** or by calling you.

■ **RULE 8:** Advertising (like most newspaper and magazine ads) that promotes your company's image will never pull immediate responses. It's not designed to do that. A promotion should pinpoint exactly what your product benefits are and tell how and when to respond to your offer. This will produce immediate responses.

Chapter 7

WHAT TO TELL YOUR LEADS TO PRE-QUALIFY THEM

KEY TERM:

Responses

To pre-qualify your leads, give prospects specifics when you introduce who you are and what you're representing. You eliminate questions and objections before they arise. But the more your lead knows, the easier it is to make a decision not to buy, without inquiring for further information from you.

Direct response marketing is the perfect medium for you to clarify and specify exactly what you want to say.

■ **RULE 9:** To generate fewer, more qualified **responses** (leads) you can:

- Tell the price of your product or service that you're selling.

- Tell your leads that a salesperson will call when they respond.

- Make them pay their own return postage. This requires more commitment and means they're really interested.

- Ask qualifying questions such as phone numbers, work address, or financial information.

■ **RULE 10:** To generate a greater quantity of leads, you will often sacrifice quality. But to get more leads you can:

- Give free gifts or offer a substantial price discount.

- Make it easy for the leads to respond with a toll-free phone number or postage paid reply envelope.

- If sales calls are not part of the follow-up, say so. The person responding will have less fear of getting a high pressure sales pitch.

- Tell prospects only enough to make them curious. Curiosity alone is a great tool to get prospects to say "Tell me more."

Part II

YOUR MARKET

Changing Names To Prospects

8. Where Do You Get Prospects?
9. How To Pick Lists That Work
10. Saving Money On Your Mailing

Chapter 8

WHERE DO YOU GET PROSPECTS?

KEY TERMS:

Compiled Lists
Response Lists
Customer Lists

Direct marketing is built on names, addresses and phone numbers. A prospect list in your marketing area should reflect the characteristics of your best clients (or potential clients).

In the course of amassing your prospect list, you'll encounter three basic types of lists: compiled lists, response lists and customer lists.

Compiled lists. Names gathered from a wide variety of general sources, like phone books, state or county filings, and published directories, are compiled lists. Public libraries have a wealth of resources available on local, regional and national levels.

Consumers can be selected by a variety of demographic characteristics such as age, income and zip code. Businesses can be selected by type of industry, number of employees, and sales volume, as well as geographical location.

Psychographic selections are also available. These include lists such as elementary school teachers or human resource directors of large companies. There are literally thousands of these types of lists available to zero in on prospects by their interests or needs.

In most cases, lead generation makes use of compiled lists because every potential customer is sought, not just those prospects who have previously responded to an offer which might indicate interest. Compiled lists, although gathered from many sources and often representing huge numbers of people aren't necessarily inaccurate. They are lists with a greater potential market for you.

Response lists. Response lists are made up of people who have actually responded to an offer. They've previously purchased from or inquired about more information from a business (even yours). The company that owns these lists may not want to release them for competitive reasons. But if the owner does make them available, the names will cost two to three times more because they reflect direct action taken by the person on the list, as opposed to potential action. These prospects should respond better to your offer than compiled names.

Surprisingly, lists of consumers and businesses that have responded to someone else's offer are generally available for rental. There are over 10,000 mailing lists available on the list market today. They include subscribers to specific magazines (such as *Guns and Ammo*, *Highlights for Children,* or anything in between), donors to certain causes (such as political contributors), sweepstakes entrants, and mail order buyers of a variety of products (from upscale merchandise to low price, high volume products).

Customer lists. Those clients that have actually made a purchase from you comprise your customer lists. These are the best pre-qualified leads for other products you have available, such as a second car, another annuity, or pruning trees in addition to cutting the lawn. Your easiest sale is to someone who already knows you and trusts you.

If you have a list of pre-qualified leads who have responded to your promotion and your noncompetitive friend also has such a list, you may want to swap leads. For example, leads of Medicare supplement buyers may be traded for leads of hearing aid buyers or business buyers of computer hardware with software buyers.

Chapter 9

HOW TO PICK LISTS THAT WORK

KEY TERMS:

List Owner, Manager, Broker
Update
Merge-Purge

No matter whether you're looking for businesses or consumers, you'll encounter good lists and some that are not so good. It's not difficult to determine if the list you want is a good list. In fact, finding a good one is as simple as asking a few specific questions.

You can rent lists from three sources. A **list owner** actually owns the list. A **list manager** sells the list for the owner.

A **list broker** supplies lists even though he or she doesn't own or manage the list.

■ **RULE 11:** When you're thinking about renting a list, ask about the original source of the list.

A marketing director once ordered a list of two generational households. He was promoting adult day care and wanted to reach middle aged children with their senior parents living at home with them. What he got was young families with adolescent children. He got households with two generations, but this was target marketing at its worst just because he never asked about the source of the list.

Don't be afraid to ask questions to make sure the list fits the profile of your prime prospects. Since one of the keys to direct mail success is regular, consistent promotion, your satisfaction with the list assures you'll be a regular customer of the list company. They'll be happy to answer all your questions.

■ **RULE 12:** Ask how often new names are added to the list, not how often it is updated. An **update** can be as simple as adding a few phone numbers. A new compilation, however, means a completely new list.

This is another matter of asking a simple question. Companies might work on cleaning their list weekly, which is good. *(See exhibit on page 40.)* But that doesn't mean any *new* names have been added to the file.

With newly compiled names, bad records should be purged or eliminated. New names should also have been added. *(See exhibit on page 41.)* These might be people buying a house in your marketing area or being hired for a corporate position responsible for purchasing your product.

Consolidated Group, Inc.
P.O. Box 9191
Framingham, MA 01701-9191

Please indicate:

☐ Keep those CGT cards and letters coming!
My address on the mailing label is:
☐ Correct   ☐ Incorrect. Please note changes.
☐ This agent is no longer with our company, but please add my name to your list. I've corrected the label.
☐ Please take my name off your list.
☐ I receive duplicate mailings from CGT. Make sure my name appears only once on your list. The duplicate name appears as:

☐ Other
Any comments? _____

Your Phone Number _____ Agent I.D. # _____

ALAN KUSHINS
KUSHINS AGENCY
16102 RED CEDAR
DALLAS, TX 75248

MLR-3

Bulk Rate
U.S. Postage
PAID
Consolidated Group

Here's a way to keep your list updated. Ask your prospects if they want to continue to receive your mail. If you don't hear from them, take them off your list.

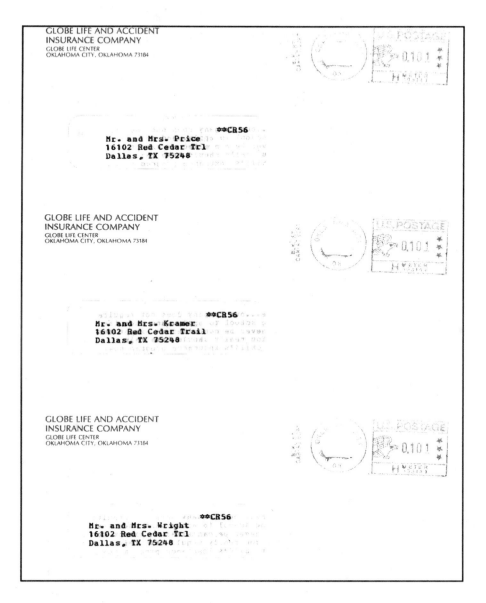

Here's an example of how postage and printing can be wasted when old names are not eliminated. These letters to three different families were received at the same address on the same day. The mailer never knew there was a problem.

■ **RULE 13:** 20% of the general population relocates every year. Businesses move and die just like people. You need to recognize that no list is perfect. Even if you compile your own list today, tomorrow it will probably be out of date.

■ **RULE 14:** Find out if telephone follow-up lists are available. Some lists have names and addresses only. Some have phone numbers for just a portion of the names. Some have phone numbers for all the names. Don't assume anything. Ask before you rent a list.

With current phone numbers in addition to current addresses, you can carry out your mailing and then follow-up with a phone call. But if you rent a list without phone numbers, you can't very well do a telephone follow-up.

Ask about a duplicate phone follow-up list when you order your original mailing list. It is usually cheaper to get the phone list as a duplicate to the original mailing list than to come back later and run it as a separate order.

■ **RULE 15:** Purge (eliminate) your current customers from your lead generation program. This not only saves you postage money, but it also keeps you from mailing a lead generation promotion to a current customer. You wouldn't want to send clients a "Let's get acquainted" offer, would you?

You can avoid this unprofessional and embarrassing situation by requesting to have your rented list sequenced in the order you prefer, such as alphabetically or by zip code. This lets you easily check against your customer file, line-by-line, to remove any current buyers from the rented list.

You can also compare the lists with a computer. It can do the **merge-purge** for you. That is, it can merge your customer file with the rented list and purge (eliminate) the duplicates.

Chapter 10

SAVING MONEY ON YOUR MAILING

KEY TERMS:

Third Class Mail
Zip Code Sequence
Carrier Route Sorting

       Postal rates continue to rise. Paper and printing costs continue to climb. You need to know where you can cut costs. By mailing to the most targeted, accurate list and by postal presorting your mail, you can save money on your direct mail programs.

Postage

■ **RULE 16:** Postage often accounts for 20% to 50% of the cost of your direct mail promotion. The question about postage that most mailers ask is, "Can you be just as effective using **third class mail** versus first class mail?" The answer is, "Maybe."

The obvious benefit of third class postage is cost. It costs you much less to mail third class. The basic cost to mail one ounce of first class is about twice the cost of third class.

However, you'll discover restrictions with **third class mail** that might far outweigh the cost considerations:

- Third class mailings require a 200-piece minimum quantity and the size and weight of each piece can't vary.

- All pieces must be in **zip code sequence** (from lowest to highest zip code).

- Third class mail always gets delivered after first class. Thus, the trade-off of postage savings might be two-week delivery for third class vs. 2-day delivery for first class.

Be careful with time sensitive offers that have expiration dates. Third class postage savings aren't worth anything if your invitation arrives after your seminar has already been given or your time limit has passed.

■ **RULE 17:** **Carrier route sorting** can save you a considerable amount of money because you're doing some of the Post Office's work. You're actually putting the mail in the postal carrier's walk route, which saves the Post Office sorting time. For doing this, they give you a substantial discount on your postage. The amount saved may easily be enough to cover the cost of renting your list. If you order names from large list companies, they can sort the names by carrier route for you.

Be careful with carrier route sorted mail. The Post Office requires certain reports and specific handling. Check with them before preparing your mail. In fact, you may want a professional mail service to take care of it for you, just to avoid any mistakes. Most business-to-business mail will not qualify for carrier route discounts because there is usually not enough concentration of mail in the carrier's walk route to meet postal requirements. If you mail most consumers in a carrier's walk route, reduced postage for carrier route sorting is common.

"Occupant" Mail

■ **RULE 18:** Don't overlook or reject the idea of addressing your mailing to "Occupant" or "Resident." It can be beneficial in certain circumstances.

Mail addressed to "Occupant" can save you money. You pay less for the list because you are not selecting by specific characteristics of an individual and you're not getting an actual name.

However, to work with an "Occupant" address, the mailing must meet a very specific criterion. It must be a general offer to which everyone on the block or in the zip code can respond.

For instance, if your business is a dry cleaner or pizza parlor, you could benefit from this type of list. In fact, if you are selling renter's insurance, mailing to all apartment dwellers in your zip code area would be smart marketing.

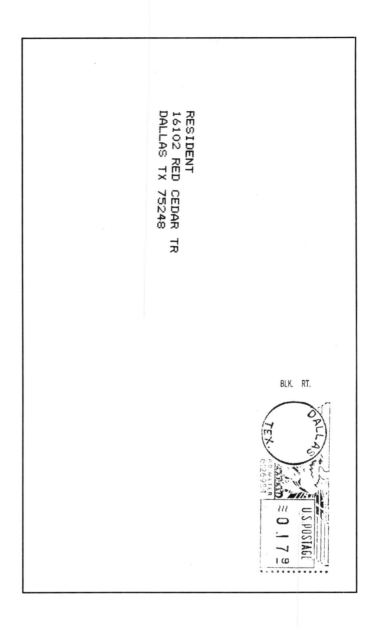

This "Resident" label was used by a local realtor. He wanted to sell my house for me. Not very personal, is it? Neither was the photo copy letter inside.

■ **RULE 19:**   Since most lead generation packages try to target prospects more specifically than everyone on the block, you can waste money renting an "Occupant" list. Without a personal name it also has the immediate perception of "junk" mail and may promptly be thrown away. *(See exhibit on page 46.)*

> *EXAMPLE*:   I once provided lists to a company selling burial insurance that had an ingenious use of the word "Occupant" in place of an actual name. They realized their mailing might reach a home near the time of a death in the family and feared offending the prospects which would create ill-will. To overcome the sensitive nature of the product, they rented addresses headed by someone over the age of 70, but then replaced the person's name with the word "Occupant" to make it appear like a general mailing.
>
> In fact, they even printed on the bottom of the mailer, "This is a mass mailing. We are sorry if it arrives at a time of grief in the household." This wording not only made it appear harmless but also made people realize they should consider burial insurance because everyone faces the inevitable.

Part III

YOUR OFFER

What To Say and How To Say It

11. The Offer
12. The Magic Words
13. Freebies — Increasing Response
14. Benefits and Features
15. Holding Attention
16. Humor — So You Think You're Funny
17. How To Put Action In Your Offer
18. Two Faces of Positioning
19. Hot Spots — The First Places Your
    Prospects Will Look
20. Headlines — Making Them Work For You

Chapter 11

THE OFFER

KEY TERMS:

Attention-Interest
Understanding-Desire
Response
Involvement Device
Hard Lead-Soft Lead

Your OFFER is the proposition that you present your prospects. Its sole purpose is to get them to contact you.

Once prospects contact you for more information, they become pre-qualified leads. Here are the major elements you must build into your offer to increase response:

Attention and Interest. The first task your offer must do is to grab the attention and interest of each person who sees it, and then hold that attention. Try reading your offer slowly and carefully aloud. Analyze it from your prospect's point of view. Does it grab your attention? Is it interesting enough to keep you reading?

Understanding and Desire. Your offer must be easily understood by each person whose attention it grabs. *(See exhibits on pages 51 and 52.)* If your prospect is initially qualified for the offer, the interest and understanding you build into the offer will create desire for more information.

Response. It's imperative that the process of responding be simple and convenient. Don't misfire by making it difficult for your prospect to contact you.

■ **RULE 20:** The more information your prospects are given, the easier it is for them to make a decision regarding your offer.

Would you rather give a prospect less information and receive a greater response, or give complete information and receive fewer, but better qualified responses?

If the size of your sales staff is limited (possibly it's just you), use what you say in your promotion to qualify your responses as much as possible. You'll come closer to reaching the cream of pre-qualified leads. However, if you manage a large sales staff, you probably want to keep the phone ringing or the cards coming in or the floor traffic busy. You can easily accomplish this by telling prospects just enough to get them to respond.

EXAMPLE: Let's say you're selling major medical insurance to small business owners with fewer than 100 employees. You'll get the most responses to your promotion with a headline like this:

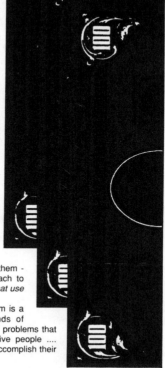

Your offer must be easily understood. This one is not.
In fact, I'm still not sure I understand what they do.

Here's an offer I *can* understand. A GUARANTEE is always powerful.

"HOW TO CUT YOUR COMPANY HEALTH INSURANCE COSTS BY 50%"

The text of the promotion would continue with something nonspecific like:

"Health care costs have risen 300% in the last two years. Find out how to cut your company's health insurance costs by 50%. Call ABC Insurance Agency today at 123-4567. Don't delay. Call today."

This type of promotion will get you the most responses because it accomplishes these tasks: 1) It gets the attention and interest of small business owners who have seen their insurance premiums continually go up; 2) It's simple and easily understood; and 3) It gives almost no details. It doesn't qualify the responses except to attract those who want to cut costs (and rest assured everyone does).

A simple reply card which repeats the headline should be included:

"☐ YES! Please let me know how I can cut my company's health insurance cost by 50%."

The check-off box doesn't add anything to the offer but it does create involvement of the reader. He or she becomes physically involved by checking the box. It is generally accepted that some form of **involvement device** will help your response.

Can you really cut respondents' health insurance costs by 50%? Maybe, maybe not. But this type of lead generation mailer gives you the chance to talk to the most prospects possible to find out.

This approach produces a **"soft" lead**; one that is not very qualified. You don't know anything specific about your inquiries and they don't really know anything specific about you either.

Getting your foot in the door is the ultimate objective of your pre-qualified lead generation program. A "soft" promotion will capture more leads than a "hard" promotion.

What do I mean by a "hard" promotion? I mean one that pulls better qualified leads for you. Here's how you could have better qualified the leads in the previous example.

"Health care costs have risen 300% in the last two years. If you employ between 25 and 100 people with no preexisting conditions, we can save you up to 50% on your health insurance costs.

"Benefits are subject to limitations and exclusions. The insurance plan is underwritten by XYZ Insurance Company of Any City, USA.

"Call ABC Insurance Agency today at 123-4567. A representative will deliver the information to you. Don't delay. Call now."

As you can see, giving the prospect more information will better qualify your lead response. A responder to the first version is more of a tire-kicker. He wants more information but is not committing to anything. If you need lots of leads to keep you or your sales staff busy, use that type of "soft" lead.

Responders to the second version are extremely interested. Not only do they know that there are limitations that might keep them from qualifying for a possible 50% reduction, but also that a salesman will show up at their door to try to help them.

This type of responder is a great pre-qualified lead! You will not get as many **hard leads** as you do soft leads. But hard leads are so ready to buy, they are like money in the bank. So which is it for you . . . a few very qualified leads or more leads that are less qualified? Your personal situation will determine the answer. The number of sales people available to work the leads and their selling ability to handle "soft" leads are important determining factors.

Chapter 12

THE MAGIC WORDS

KEY TERMS:

Free
New

While you were growing up, you probably learned the magic words "please" and "thank you." Now, as you mature in lead generation, you'll discover the value of the magic words "FREE" and "NEW."

Remember, one of the best things about direct response marketing is that you can test your offers for more effective wording. Very often, using one of the Magic Words will produce better responses for you.

If you are 60 or older, wouldn't you show up for free testing?

■ **RULE 21:** With few exceptions, you will see that an offer with something "Free" generates more responses than the same offer with nothing "Free." *(See exhibit on page 57.)*

The concept of "**Free**" can be stated in several different ways. Which of these ways to say "free" do you think will generate the most responses?

1. Half price!
2. 50% Off!
3. Buy one, get one free.

According to Bob Stone, a noted authority on direct mail marketing, "Buy one, get one free" pulls better than the other two. How much better would you guess? A full 40% better! Why does it out perform the others? Because of the magic word "free."

■ **RULE 22:** The word "**New**" is one that always gets people's attention. The American public is constantly taught by the fashion industry to want the very latest, whatever that may be.

One of my first jobs when I was in college was selling shoes. I remember a particular day I tried a technique that taught me the value of the word "New."

I was able to get a woman to come back into the store, after she literally had one foot out the door. I asked her, "Would you like to see something new we just got in for fall?" It was just too hard for her to resist. She not only came back into the store but also bought the shoes. What a great way to learn the value of the magic word "New."

Chapter 13

FREEBIES — INCREASING RESPONSE

KEY TERMS:

Cost per Lead
Cost per Sale
Freebie Junkies

Many lead generation offers give the reader something "free" to increase response. In fact, you can lower your cost per lead enough to more than pay for the give-away items.

Whether related to the product or not, free gifts pull in the responses. Here are "Free" give-aways that can help you increase response:

- *Free Information.* Free brochures, booklets, video or audio tapes.

- *Free Analysis.* For instance, a free review of your personal finances or a free dental checkup.

- *Free Subscription.* People enjoy having access to information. They'll accept a free subscription to almost anything, like your newsletter for example.

- *Free Food.* Giving away food (such as free refreshments at your seminar) always draws a strong response. Everyone can appreciate food!

■ **RULE 23:** Anything given away must be analyzed for its impact on **cost per lead** and **cost per sale**.

I've used give-away items that have doubled the response rate to promotions. No other changes were necessary for the dramatic increase . . . just a "freebie."

One of our mailers had been pulling an average of 3% response which at $300 per thousand pieces mailed, yielded a cost of $10 per lead. By increasing the responses to 6%, the lead cost came down to $5 each. Even with the added charge of $1 for the give-away item (in this case it was an information booklet), the end result was that we reduced the overall cost per lead from $10 to $6! Freebies do work.

■ **RULE 24:** Giving away something related to your product or service will generate responses from people who are interested in what you are selling. *(See exhibits on pages 61 and 62.)*

BULK RATE
U.S. POSTAGE
PAID
PERMIT NO. 820
LINCOLN, NE

Yours Free — A 20-page Financial Guide covering stocks and bonds, CDs, IRAs, tax shelters, and how they fit into a balanced personal financial plan.

** CAR-RT SORT ** CR56
9101AMMA912171 2063672
ALLYN R KRAMER
16102 RED CEDAR TRL **
DALLAS TX 75248

IDS
An American Express company

IDS ties in their Financial Guide give-away perfectly with the financial products they are marketing.

State Mutual Companies

440 Lincoln Street
Worcester, MA 01605

Allyn Kramer
16102 Red Cedar Tr
Dallas, TX 75248

Dear Executive:

Let us introduce you to the new, pocket-sized Rand McNally Road Atlas. The compact size makes it handy to keep in the glove compartment, desk drawer or brief case for ready reference.

With this useful gift you will also receive a booklet that contains information of special importance for you and your family.

Written in clear, easy-to-read terms, it reveals:

   The advantages to you and your family of an Estate Plan

   Tax information that may save your family thousands of dollars

   The cost of ignorance (or neglect) in accumulating and distributing a personal estate.

You will agree this information should be required reading for business and professional people interested in their own and their family's financial future.

Just mail the lower portion of this page. Your pocket-sized Rand McNally Road Atlas and the Estate Savings information will reach you promptly and without obligation.

                              Sincerely,

                              Arthur H. Alie

                              Arthur H. Alie
                              Vice President

- Detach on dotted line -

_____Yes, I would like to receive the useful free gift and the information mentioned in your letter.

I'm also interested in   ☐ Lower Premiums for Non-Smokers
                             ☐ Estate Planning Information
                             ☐ Tax Favored Products
017 0706 I29 O   ☐ Other _____
Allyn Kramer
16102 Red Cedar Tr
Dallas, TX 75248

            Daytime Phone No. _____

What does a road atlas have to do with estate planning? Rand McNally probably sold plenty of road maps, but I'm not sure State Mutual Companies did very well.

If the give-away is linked to your product or service, you should have fewer problems with **"freebie junkies"** — people who respond to get anything free, but are not qualified and will never have an interest in your product or service.

In the example of the information booklet, representatives delivering the freebie expressed delight with the ease they were able to transition or flow into their sales presentation. Because of the tie-in of their product to the booklet, many were able to close more sales per presentation, improving their **cost per sale**.

In the worst case, the close rate remained the same as without the freebie. But with more leads they were still further ahead than without using a give-away.

One of the newest lead generation give-aways is an instructional video cassette for private viewing. This tool gives prospects the opportunity to hear your presentation without you being present. It provides a more relaxed atmosphere for consideration of your offer.

I have to smile when recalling how my father-in-law, Herb Bauer, bought an insurance policy from an agent who simply asked if he had a VCR (70% of households do). Then the agent wanted to know if he could drop off a VCR tape that evening and he would come by in a couple of days to pick it up.

After two days the agent called to find out when he could get the tape. He also politely asked if Herb had any questions. No, he didn't. Was he interested in the insurance policy? Yes, he was. The agent not only picked-up the tape, he also received a check. The video did all the work. Of course the video tape was very professionally prepared by the agent's company.

EXAMPLE: Let's say you are hand-delivering a free gift and want to make a full sales presentation at that time. Here's how you make the most of the situation.

The first thing you must do is to let the respondents know you've brought the gift with you. You can even show it to them. But *don't* hand it over. Set it aside and launch into your presentation. That way they know they'll get the gift and they won't be distracted wondering about it while you are talking.

Give them the gift only after you've completed your presentation. If you hand it over before you begin, they're likely to be examining it while you are trying to explain your offer. Your words will be lost because they won't be paying attention to you.

Chapter 14

BENEFITS AND FEATURES

KEY TERMS:

Benefits
Features

One of the most important differences between direct response marketing and awareness or image advertising is the difference between benefits and features.

Benefits are the advantages buyers receive when owning your product or service (such as security, convenience, or prestige). **Features** are the particulars of the product or service that make it different from its competition (such as price or color).

If you want immediate response, talk benefits to the reader in your advertising copy. If you want to create awareness for possible future impact, talk about features of your product.

Here's a simple example:

Feature	Benefit
Now only $19.95!	Save $5.00

See the difference? The feature states a point about the product — the price. The benefit tells what the price will do for your prospects — save them money. *(See exhibits on pages 67, 68, and 69.)*

Here's another example:

Feature	Benefit
We have 20 years experience.	Discover the great quality others have relied on for 20 years.

It is much easier to write about features because you're only describing the product or service. It takes a great deal of thought to translate features into benefits for your prospects and move them to action.

THE

Farmers Insurance Group OF COMPANIES

Matt Lohoefer Insurance Agency
9500 Forest Lane #100
Dallas, Texas 75243
(214) 343-9497

Allyn Kramer
16102 Red Cedar Trl
Dallas, TX 75248

Dear Allyn,

THIS LETTER COULD SAVE YOU MONEY!
Farmers Insurance is offering LOW-LOW Rates on Auto & Homeowners!

Yes, that is correct and you could save as much as 25% off your current rate. I will call in the near future to personally give you a quote but please call before your renewal and save. We also work with your Mortgage Company if necessary.

Farmers intends to be the #1 Insurance Company and I also intend to be one of the Best Agents in North Texas. Please consider the savings and the excellent service that I offer. THERE IS A DIFFERENCE!

Please give me a call at 343-9497 anytime for a no obligation quote. We have VERY COMPETITIVE RATES ON AUTO INSURANCE! Farmers will also give an additional 7% discount on your homeowners if we insure your autos also.

Sincerely,

Matt Lohoefer
Farmers Insurance Group of Companies

P.S.   Our new office is at LBJ & Forest Lane!

P.S.S.   Yes we do beat Allstate & State Farm on price with broader and more complete coverage!

P.S.S.S. If you have been cancelled please call and join the fastest growing company in the United States.

Here's a benefit everyone wants . . . saving money. This is a great response-getting offer.

Great Expectations

"We make meeting people easier."

*We make meeting quality single people easier.
You won't waste time on blind dates
or meet the wrong types
with our video viewing approach.*

Dear Single,

Finding the time to meet new, interesting single people and develop special relationships gets more difficult every year.

We're just not exposed to enough of the right kind of fine quality singles. We're locked into our work, our neighborhood and our limited circle of friends. The busier we get, the less time we have to look, and the fewer options we have. So, hoping for the lucky chance encounter that rarely occurs, we sometimes settle for second best. And that just isn't good enough. Not anymore.

Great Expectations offers a better way. We've helped thousands of successful, selective singles meet and begin fulfilling relationships. In fact, our success has been featured on shows like *Phil Donahue*, *Oprah*, *Sally Jessy Raphael*, *CBS's 48 Hours*, and reported in top national magazines such as *Newsweek*, *Glamour*, *Ms.*, *The New Republic* and *Fortune*.

Our exclusive video viewing approach lets you screen, at your leisure, our extensive Library of other selective singles...over 90,000 Members nationwide...the world's largest selection. In comfortable privacy, you'll see and hear them in relaxed video conversations. You then select whom you'd like to meet.

It's a wonderfully efficient -- and dignified -- way to find the kind of person you prefer to socialize with, before you agree to meet with them. So you don't waste your precious time on blind dates or with losers.

To learn more about how you can find the fulfilling relationship that may be missing in your life, simply complete and return the confidential Profile Form that's on the back of this letter. Or call your local Centre today. The information is free and without obligation.

The right potential partner -- you might otherwise never meet -- may be waiting for you in our Library right now!

Respectfully,

Jeffrey Ullman
Jeffrey Ullman
Founder and President

JU:rs

P.S.   Please complete and return your confidential Profile Form today. Explore your options, and find out how easy it is for you to meet other successful, busy singles who want to find that special relationship.

The benefit for interested singles is clear: this method is easier and saves time.

A MEMBER OF THE SEARS FINANCIAL NETWORK

COLDWELL BANKER ◻

The Home Sellers®

Dear: Property Owners and Friends

First I would like to introduce myself. My name is Don
Davis and I work for COLDWELL BANKER residential real estate.
My office is located at Preston road and McCallum road or
just north of Campbell road at Preston. I have decided to
work in your area and hope I can do the best job possible
for my clients and customers. I have selected this beautiful area
because of its proximaty to my office and the distintive features
and style of homes. I hope I can meet each and every person in
my marketing area. I also hope that property values increase
in this particular area as well as the rest of the metroplex.
I think that property values in this area are holding relatively
strong compared to the rest of the country. I would like to be
well versed in property in the area so that I might be of help
to the public. My goal in real estate is to help obtain your
goal. If you have any questions about real estate, please do
not hesitate to call. My message center number is 250-1057.
I would appreciate your current or future bussiness and will
help you to the best of my ability. If there is anything I can
do to help you in your line of work, I will happy to help. If
you have a friend who is trying to sell a home or buy a home,
please give them my number. I am sure I can help them. Thanks
for your help and good luck. May you have a prosperous 1991.

Sincerely: Don Davis

Donald E. Davis Jr.

If your property is currently listed with a real estate broker, please disregard
this offer; it is not our intention to solicit the offerings of other real estate
brokers. We are happy to work with them and cooperate fully.

Where's the benefit? This fellow wrote an entire letter
without naming one thing he's going to do for his prospect.

Chapter 15

HOLDING ATTENTION

KEY TERMS:

Testimonials
Case Histories
Copy

Once you have captured the reader's attention, you must hold onto that attention. Several tools are available for accomplishing this task.

■ **RULE 25:** **Testimonials** and **case histories** lend credibility to your offer. If you want to use these, don't rely on just one. The secret to using them successfully is to bombard your readers with as many testimonials as possible.

Why so many? The fewer you present, the more skeptical readers become. You are less likely to be convincing. (Did your friend write it?) Ask satisfied clients for written endorsements. Use these testimonials as often as possible. They'll give your prospects the perception that you are as good as you say you are. It's more believable when someone else says it.

■ **RULE 26:** Write the way you talk. According to Johathan Kozol, in his book, *Illiterate America*, about 45% of the adult population reads at the 8th grade level or below. Use short words, short sentences, and short paragraphs, even though you may have a long letter.

It's usually very easy to tell if your text (or **"copy"** as it's called in advertising) has been written by an amateur writer. Professionals work to communicate ideas easily. Amateurs work to impress the readers with their vocabulary. Big words scare off readers. Little words make them feel comfortable.

If you try writing the promotion yourself, pretend you're explaining your offer to an eighth grader. Use these tools:

1. <u>Underline important words</u>.

2. **Put them in bold type.**

3. • List points with a bullet.

4.   Indent it.

How To Make People Line Up And Beg You To Take Their Money!

FROM: Kenneth B. Hough
Thursday: 5:30 P.M.

Dear Friend,

As you can see, I have attached a copper penny to the top of this letter. Why have I done this? Actually, there are two reasons:

1. I have something very important to tell you and I needed some way to make sure this letter gets your attention.

2. And, secondly, since what I have to tell you concerns money, I felt that some sort of little "financial eyecatcher" was appropriate.

Why am I so excited? The answer is simple: You see, I have discovered a way to make more money in a day than most people make in a week! I'm dead serious. And, guess what else? What I have discovered is so hot it actually makes people stand in line to give you their money!

I'm not kidding. This is, by far, the most amazing money-making opportunity you have ever seen. In fact, it involves all three of the hottest businesses of the last ten years which are computers, video cameras and instant pictures!

Listen carefully. What I'm talking about is the amazing CASI Computer Portrait System. Have you ever seen one? Believe me, they really draw a crowd! In fact, whenever one of our operators puts one in a shopping center, a store, a county fair or anywhere else, they attract people (and money) like iron-filings are attracted to a magnet! And, it's no wonder. You see, this remarkable system turns out an incredible lifelike video portrait in just seconds and then you can immediately transfer that picture onto a T-shirt, a baseball cap, a poster, a puzzle, a pillowcase or even a BBQ apron and probably, at least, a dozen other items.

Sounds neat, doesn't it? And, it's so easy, even a child can run it. But, believe me, the profits are not kid stuff. In fact, we have plenty of people, just like yourself, who are taking home hundreds of dollars

(Go to Page 2)

An actual penny glued to the letter gets attention.

5. **B**egin your paragraph with a large capital.

6. End an incomplete thought or question with an ellipsis . . .

7. . . . Lead into a thought with an ellipsis.

■ **RULE 27:** Be specific (such as "70 Rules"). Be immediate (such as "Call us now for free information."). People like numbers and they don't like to wait. *(See exhibit on page 72.)*

Chapter 16

HUMOR — SO YOU THINK YOU'RE FUNNY

KEY TERM:

Setup and Punch

Humor and cuteness are dangerous. Why? Because they can easily be misunderstood and cause confusion. Or worse, they can be interpreted as offensive. Remember that confusion causes the reader to stop reading. And offensiveness can guarantee your competition gets the business.

■ **RULE 28:** To be successful, humor must touch virtually every reader. By targeting a specific group, you have a better chance of succeeding with humor than addressing a general audience.

If you're determined to use humor, don't try to make people laugh. Try to make them smile. It's easier and you'll be more successful with it. *(See exhibits on pages 76 and 77.)*

Most humor is a logical premise followed by an illogical conclusion. In comedy terms, this is called the **setup and the punch**. In order to work, the punch must be exaggerated enough to separate and stand out from the initial logic.

In other words, if you're going to attempt humor, make it obvious. And since your job is to get people to respond favorably to you, not to entertain them, recognize that most people will respond favorably only if they understand you.

Here's an attempt at humor that I enjoyed.

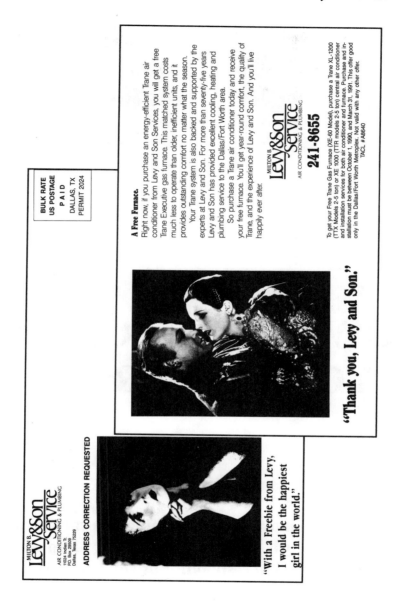

Humor is not easy to do, as this example points out. At least it didn't make me smile.

Chapter 17

HOW TO PUT ACTION IN YOUR OFFER

KEY TERM:

Action Verbs

The most important thing you can do to add spice to your copy is use words that move, jump and excite your readers to respond! But you need to know which words will accomplish this.

For instance, if you were mailing a package to business executives you could use, "We will expedite your request", and they would likely respond. However, if your mailing were to senior citizens, your call-to-action ("expedite") would likely fall flat compared to, "We'll rush your information to you."

■ **RULE 29:** When you write, look for **action verbs**.

Which moves you more?

"Here is an offer for you" . . . or . . . "Wake up to this opportunity"

Written words can have flair just like an animated speech. Here are examples of how to make words more active and colorful:

DULL	ALIVE
"a new source"	"a refreshing new source"
"you'll like"	"you'll enjoy"
"ability to"	"with the power to"
"efficient"	"strong, business-like approach"
"performs"	"sparkles"

Avoid inactive and boring words like: be, are, have, has. However, words like the ones below will also help you gain and hold your reader's attention:

Save	Now	Look	Watch
Send	Jump	Excite	Create
Enjoy	Succeed	Grow	See
Hurry	Imagine	Today	First-time
Urgent	Own	Order	Satisfy
Important	Reach	Join	Notice

P.S. Don't forget about *Free* and *New*.

In fact, before you send your package to the printer, take the final draft of your letter and brochure and lay them out in front of you. With a yellow marker, highlight all the verbs. Watch for the action and inaction. Look out for repetition and make changes as appropriate. You might keep a thesaurus (dictionary of synonyms) handy to help you find replacement words. *(See exhibit on page 81.)*

■ **RULE 30:** Contractions help your readers hear your words as though they were being spoken. So, always use words like:

we're	instead of	we are
can't	instead of	can not
won't	instead of	will not
you'll	instead of	you will

CHICAGO · DALLAS

March 6, 1990

Allyn Kramer
Senior Citizens Marketing Group
9319 LBJ Freeway, Suite 120
Dallas, Texas 75243

Dear Ms. Kramer:

Allow me to present the services of Michael Edwards Communications,
a refreshing new source for creative help I'm sure you'll feel comfortable
calling upon anytime you have a direct marketing project.

You see, we specialize in direct response vehicles that are remarkable
for their originality. And their power to lift response. But,
the first thing you'll probably notice at the onset of our relationship
is that we're a creative group with some strong, business-like disciplines.

A project, for instance, starts out with our discovering everything
we can about the product or service, the target market, the objective
– and putting it all down on paper in what we call a creative plan.
Essentially, it's a working plan for all concerned, ultimately allowing
us to arrive at creative strategies that are valid regarding both
marketing objectives and production realities.

The result? Fresh tests that win.

Because as you probably already perceive, nothing comes off the
shelf here. We dig into the offering. Come up with its unique
selling proposition that separates itself from the competition.
And deliver it on time. Custom made, hand-fitted and polished to
a shine.

Whatever you need, creative strategy help, concept development,
copy, art direction, photography, illustration, print production
coordination – we're a singular source you can call upon anytime.
I think you'll be glad you've found us.

That's why I'll be calling you personally in a few days, to see
if there's any thing you'd like to explore further in our array
of services, either for an immediate project or perhaps one down
the road a bit.

Yours truly,

DJ Compton
Vice President/Account Supervisor

Here's a dynamite letter loaded with action words and
phrases. Plenty of thought went into this one.

Chapter 18

TWO FACES OF POSITIONING

KEY TERMS:

Physical Positioning
Viewpoint Positioning

Positioning for our purpose means two different things. They're both important enough to deserve your attention.

Physical Positioning. The physical position that words occupy on a page can call attention to them. However, be careful about the meaning you want to convey.

A classic example is the letter sent by a company informing its customers of a newly upgraded service. The accidental position of the words must have had a drastic and horrible result to the company. (They're no longer in business.) The opening line of the letter read: ". . . no longer in business . . ." The second line in the letter completed the thought.

National Referral Systems, Inc.

SPECIAL BULLETIN

National Referral Systems is no longer in business . . . just to coordinate direct mail programs for the insurance industry. We have expanded our service, and our facilities!

Over the past five years, our organization has been recognized nationally as a leader in providing direct mail programs, primarily for the insurance industry.

With our expansion, we can now assist you with an entire range of marketing services including:

- ★ Layout and Design of Mail Packages
- ★ Graphic Arts and Typesetting
- ★ Printing (4-Color Process, Continuous Form, Impact and Laser)
- ★ Mail Processing, and
- ★ Name Lists!

We are now a growing force in the name list brokerage business, representing many of the nation's top list compilers. As a broker, **N.R.S.I.** has access to a consumer file that has 130 million consumers, by exact age, and this file contains 76 million heads of household. Many other files are also available.

N.R.S.I. will provide you with a "one stop" solution to your marketing needs, so give us a call, toll free. We look forward to hearing from you.

Sincerely,

National Referral Systems, Inc.

As you can see, physical positioning had a major impact on the meaning of that sentence. Many readers stopped after the first line. They started calling other suppliers to replace the one they thought had gone out of business.

Viewpoint Positioning. The other type of positioning relates to point of view. It gives the reader the impression of who it is you believe to be most important. Who do you see as more important in this example? "We've improved our service and we're ready to show just how good we really are!"

If it seems to you that the company has a very high opinion of itself, you're right. The word "we" was used three times, while "you" wasn't used at all.

■ **RULE 31:** The word YOU is almost as magic as FREE and NEW. Use it again and again. ("You" helps sell benefits because it puts the product or service in the prospect's perspective.) It creates a one-to-one relationship between you and your reader.

You may have great prospects, but they simply couldn't care less about how great you think your company or product is. They want to know only what you can do for them . . . how you can help them meet a need . . . how you can help them solve a problem . . . how you can save them money.

Chapter 19

HOT SPOTS — THE FIRST PLACES YOUR PROSPECTS WILL LOOK

KEY TERM:

Hot Spots

The strange but simple truth about writing your own direct mail package is that if you can follow the rules, you can succeed with your own writing. Understanding hot spots is one of the most important rules to follow.

■ **RULE 32: Hot Spots** are the first places your prospects will look. Thus, they're the most important places in your package. They're where you must succeed if prospects are to eventually become pre-qualified leads. *(See exhibit on page 87.)*

Hot spots are these places:

- Outside envelope
- Brochure headline
- Inside address of the letter (who it's going to)
- Signature line of the letter (who it's coming from)
- Post script of the letter (the final word)

In these places you attract attention; give your major benefit; mention as many magic words as you can; and qualify your reader. If the prospect will read anything, it'll be in these five places. This is where you pull that reader into the rest of your message.

Once you've constructed these lines, most of your creative work is over. Everything is built on the concepts given in these places. If your readers get no farther than these places, at least they'll know what you're offering. They should be able to accept or reject your offer based on what you tell them in these hot spots.

My all time favorite Hot Spot. How could I
resist opening it? It was a subscription offer
from *Advertising Age* magazine.

Chapter 20

HEADLINES — MAKING THEM WORK FOR YOU

Drive down any highway in America and you'll see billboards — a very strong visual and a short headline. Walk past any magazine or newspaper rack and see what catches your eye. Headlines are what jump out at you.

Your headline should grab your reader's attention. It shouts your benefits or offer in just a few words.

■ **RULE 33:** How large can your headline be? Very large. In fact, it can take up to a third of the ad space or brochure panel.

■ **RULE 34:** There are six different kinds of headlines:

1. Commanding:

This is the battering ram of headlines. There's no subtlety or finesse. It's direct and to the point. It commands your prospect to contact you. *(See exhibit on page 90.)*

"Earn 50% more commissions this year."

2. How-to:

This headline is powerful. It promises a big payoff to the person who responds to the offer.

"How to earn more and work less." *"How to triple your reading speed."*

3. Question:

A question that also implies a benefit is an excellent headline concept.

"Will you protect the estate you've worked a lifetime to build?"

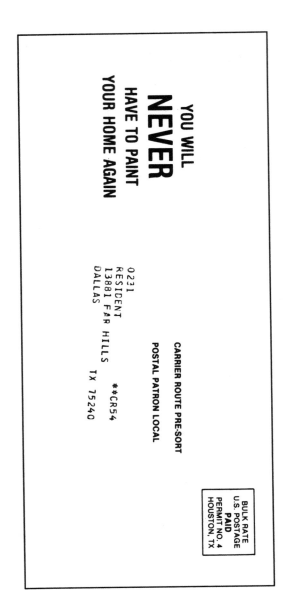

Here's a commanding headline.

4. News:

The promise of the benefits contained in something new, something recently discovered, is a magnetic pull on most people. Promise your major benefit in the style of a newspaper headline.

"Stay healthy and live longer. New fitness plan protects your greatest asset—your health."

5. Testimonials:

When someone else says it, it's more believable.

"Your results were fantastic! Keep up the good work."

6. Intrigue:

A headline can grab a reader's curiosity. *(See exhibit on page 92.)*

"They laughed when I sat down at the piano."

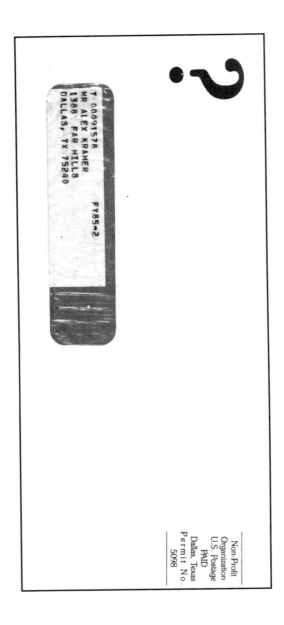

The ultimate of intrigue. It was a donor solicitation
from a public television station.

Part IV

THE PACKAGE

Your Direct Mail Workhorse

21. The Look of Your Mailer —
    Its Visual Personality
22. Response Device — Mail Me In
23. Follow-Up Letters
24. Working With An Ad Agency

Chapter 21

THE LOOK OF YOUR MAILER — ITS VISUAL PERSONALITY

KEY TERM:

40-40-20 Rule

Your goal in direct response marketing is to get pre-qualified leads. Your first objective, though, is to get your mailer opened. That's half the battle. The look and visual personality are therefore important.

■ **RULE 35:** Because of today's mailbox glut, your promotion needs to stand out in the stack of mail. Oversized mailers, bright colors, important-looking envelopes, and benefit copy all help get your reader's attention and interest. Look at these different types of mailers:

The Bureaucrat. This almost always gets opened. It might be a telegram look-alike or something else official looking. This tactic is often employed in business-to-business direct mail to assure that the piece takes a direct route to your prospect and isn't opened by the secretary. *(See exhibit on page 96.)*

Consumers are also attracted by what might appear to be an official document from a law firm or government agency. These tactics are effective in getting the mailer opened. But when the true purpose of the piece is discovered, your offer must be strong enough to overcome the negative impact of your prospect feeling deceived.

Official bureaucratic wording includes "Official document enclosed" and "Registration certificate enclosed." The return address might be that of an official sounding name. Something that sounds like a law firm, such as "Winston and Hughes."

The Promise. Would you respond to a promise of money, a special invitation, or a free gift? The promise suggests your dream may have come true. *(See exhibit on page 97.)*

Window envelopes, with what appears to be a check showing through, imply the promise. Invitation size envelopes with fine paper also imply the promise. Outside envelope copy like "You may have already won!" and "You're invited" imply the promise.

The Big Blank. Consistently, a plain white envelope with no company name or teaser copy, will get opened by the recipient. Curiosity alone will get your mailer opened.

The Teacher. Newsletters and booklets that are primarily educational and secondarily commercial will pay off. By educating people, you establish credibility.

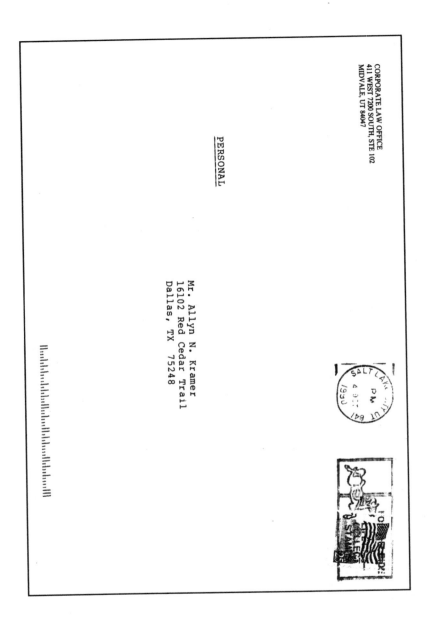

This *Bureaucrat* turned out to be an invitation to a free seminar on protecting your assets. The speaker had a "JD" degree.

The *Promise* of a good looking lawn.

But your promotion needs to end with an "Oh . . . by the way" approach, almost as an afterthought. Mention that if they would like more information, they should contact you. Your educational message by itself is image advertising. If your prospect has a way to respond to you, it becomes lead generation. Chapter 22 explores different types of response devices.

■ **RULE 36:** What works today will eventually lose its punch. For your mailings to continue to be productive, you must continue to test new ideas against your standard mailer.

Often something as simple as a change of paper color or envelope can freshen up a mailing format, even if the message doesn't change.

■ **RULE 37:** Concentrate on using the right list and promoting the right offer. The look of the mailer is secondary.

This is called the **40-40-20 Rule.** 40% of the success of your promotion comes from attacking the right market — your list. And 40% of your success is from the offer — the hook that grabs your readers. But only 20% of the success of the promotion emerges because of the look of your mailer.

Many people tend to get bogged down with the creative side of their mail package. Don't worry about artistic perfection. It's better to get your piece put together with your best offer and mailed to your best market than to fret over whether or not the appearance is perfect.

Chapter 22

RESPONSE DEVICE — MAIL ME IN

KEY TERM:

Project Code

You can't get a good response unless you have a good response device. The means by which your pre-qualified prospects respond can range from a reply card to a phone number. Whatever you use, it must be prominent and easy to use.

■ **RULE 38:** Give your prospects different opportunities to respond favorably. You might have one option on the reply card say, "YES! Call me immediately." A second option might say, "I'm not sure. Send me more information." *(See exhibit on page 100.)*

PULL

NEW YORK LIFE

MELVIN P ISAACS CLU

▼ Please indicate necessary address changes. ▼

CAR-RT PRESORT   **CB54
Allyn R. Kramer
13881 Far H1 Dr.
Dallas TX 75240

D27 MPI00   HL

**YES, I would like
to receive the
FREE GIFT and further
information on:**

- ☐ Estate Conservation
- ☐ Family Protection
- ☐ Mortgage Protection
- ☐ Education Plan
- ☐ Retirement Income
- ☐ Business Life
  Insurance
- ☐ Group Insurance
- ☐ IRA/Keogh/TSA Plan
- ☐ Pension Plan
- ☐ Health Insurance
- ☐ Other _____

Birth date _____

No stamp or signature necessary to mail this card.

1119(781)

Too many options on a reply card are confusing. When prospects have to stop and think about your offer, you will get fewer inquiries. They might put it aside to study later, but never get around to it. Simple and easy are critical elements to the best response rate.

■ **RULE 39:** You'll get the quickest responses by offering a phone number to call. Prospects who call are the best leads since they want to talk now, not sometime after they mail in the reply card and you get around to answering it. *(See exhibit on page 102.)*

■ **RULE 40:** Remember to include a **project code** so you can keep track of how many responses you get from each mailing. This can be as simple as a letter or number unique to each mailing that identifies the type of mailer, specific list, time of year, or other variables you want to track or analyze. You can place this project code on the peel-n-stick label that comes back with the reply card or print it on the reply card itself.

Tally the project codes as cards are received to determine which one pulls the most responses. The same technique applies to phone inquiries. Assign a special extension number to each mailer or list you want to test. Then have your receptionist tally each call by the extension number requested.

Always use a response device: a reply card, return envelope, or a toll-free phone number to call. Traditional mail-back response devices include:

- *Three-panel mailer.* A standard letter-size sheet folded twice. The bottom third panel is perforated as a reply card to tear off and mail back.

- *Classic mailer.* A letter, brochure, reply card, and return envelope inserted into an outside envelope. Often the label is applied to the reply card with the address showing through the widow of the outside envelope.

- *Double postcard.* A two-panel postcard that is perforated in the middle so one side can be a response card.

Here's a good example of combining a reply card with general advertising. This was inserted into an envelope with offers from other service and retail businesses in their trading area.

Always give your prospects an easy, simple, and quick way to inquire. That's not as automatic as it might seem. Even after 15 years in the business, I once got caught flatfooted. I became wrapped up in the cleverness of one of my own promotions and how quickly it had to get in the mail. It wasn't until we started to analyze the lack of response that I discovered I had forgotten to include our address and phone number on the response card. That hurt, emotionally as well as financially.

Chapter 23

FOLLOW-UP LETTERS

A follow-up letter can be one of the most important steps in gaining a customer. It shows your prospects that you're interested in them. It indicates that you're willing to work for their business (not just send them a standard packet). And it keeps them from forgetting your product or service even if they don't buy right away.

The follow-up letter can come immediately after your phone conversation as a thank you for the opportunity to introduce your product or service. Or it can come $1^1/2$ to 2 weeks after the initial material (brochure or price quote) is sent.

How many follow-up letters you send depends on the importance of the prospect. How you value the prospect depends on how close they are to buying or if you think they represent a large dollar potential.

Send follow-up letters to important prospects two weeks after mailing the initial information packet. Then another follow-up letter two weeks after that. In some cases, when you think the prospect represents significant potential, send a third letter one month after the second one.

At some point, you have to judge if you're making a pest of yourself. That's when to stop. But even then, keep them on your general promotion list so they'll hear from you periodically, along with everyone else on that list.

■ **RULE 41:** Remember these key points in your follow-up letter: Spelling, Thank you, Information, Friends.

- *Spelling.* Take the time to know how to spell your prospect's name correctly. It's simply an insult to misspell the name of someone you're trying to persuade.

- *Thank you.* Start and end every communication with a "thank you." This phrase and the prospect's name are two things he or she can never hear enough.

- *Information.* After you have provided the information requested, don't oversell. The follow-up letter can restate your main points, but it's not where you should present your entire story over again.

- *Friends.* Be yourself and be friendly. Remember to write the way you talk.

Chapter 24

WORKING WITH AN AD AGENCY

KEY TERM:

Clip Art

Many direct marketers write and coordinate their own projects. They get illustrations from clip art books and "borrow" layout ideas from pieces they've received in the mail. Then, as success grows, they hire an advertising agency to take over the production of the art and write their copy.

Clip art is the name applied to generic art that you can cut out of books purchased from art supply shops. It's tedious and time consuming, but many firms succeed because of this effort.

Working with an ad agency can signal a noticeable and significant improvement in the quality of the mailings in terms of professional appearance. However, it can also signal a decline in response or a loss of focus on the goal.

■ **RULE 42:** If you decide to hire an ad agency, be certain it employs experts in direct response marketing.

Most agencies are excellent image makers, but they don't know how to execute a direct mail lead generation program. Image makers believe pretty advertising is what you want. But immediate responses are what you know you need. Hire an agency that knows how to get responses. *(See exhibit on page 108.)*

Don't be fooled or impressed by the "look" of image advertising. It is a different tool for a different job. Some of the plainest-looking mailers have pulled the best response for me. And some of the most beautiful (and expensive) have fallen flat on their faces. Remember, if you use the right list and promote the right offer, the look of the piece is secondary.

This over-sized postcard reproduced a picture of the realtor's billboard. Image advertising? Yes. Response-getting? No.

Part V

TELEMARKETING

The Fastest Way
To Reach Pre-Qualified Prospects

25. Say Hello To Prospects
26. The Conversation — What To Say
    and How To Say It
27. Credibility — What Not To Do
28. Forbidden Phrases

Chapter 25

SAY HELLO TO PROSPECTS

Telemarketing can be used alone or in conjunction with direct mail. Once you have your prospect list or pre-qualified direct mail responses, the telephone is the surest, quickest way to make lots of contacts.

To most people, a cold call is an annoying interruption of their dinner, favorite TV show, or other personal time. And their objections are justified. The telemarketer who calls during these moments should expect a high rejection rate. There is a better, more productive way.

■ **RULE 43:** The easiest way to approach telemarketing is with a follow-up to your pre-qualified direct mail inquiries.

Pre-qualified leads have asked you to tell them more. When you phone, immediately explain that you're calling because they requested more information. This assures that you will have the prospect's attention and interest.

I always tell the person right up front that my call is in response to their inquiry. This obviously avoids wasting time and overcomes any natural resistance that could have been encountered if I had been thought of as "just another salesman."

■ **RULE 44:** There's a right time and a wrong time to call.

- Consumer prospects should be called in the evenings (after dinner time) and on weekends.

- Senior citizen retirees are best reached in morning rather than in the evening. Experts suggest seniors generally rise early and retire early.

- Business owners and managers can often be reached directly before or after regular business hours or on Saturday mornings. The idea is to catch them when secretaries are not in the office to screen their calls.

When you encounter a secretary or receptionist, use the executive's first name to imply that your prospect knows you personally. This helps reduce the receptionist's sales resistance designed to protect the boss.

Chapter 26

THE CONVERSATION – WHAT TO SAY AND HOW TO SAY IT

How do you know what words to use in your presentation? First, do your homework. Know your target market well enough to know what kind of conversation will gain acceptance. Whether you're calling personally or your telemarketing staff is doing the talking, know your prospect's language.

If you're phoning teenagers, you would certainly be more relaxed and less business-like than talking to corporate professionals. I've been told that talking to senior citizens requires a warmup period that could take several calls over several days.

■ **RULE 45:** Work from a prepared outline, not a script. Few people can sound spontaneous and believable while reading a script. An outline gives you the information you need and still lets you sound natural.

Think about the calls you've gotten. Did the presentation sound spontaneous (a sign of a good telemarketer) or did it sound "canned" (a sign of a script reader)?

■ **RULE 46:** Always smile into the phone. As odd as it sounds, your smile will carry over into your voice. Prospects will perceive you as friendlier.

■ **RULE 47:** Stick to one idea and be brief. As soon as you start bringing in unnecessary details, you're sunk, especially with busy executives.

■ **RULE 48:** Use the prospect's name throughout your conversation. It invites friendliness.

■ **RULE 49:** Since most people don't understand technical terms, using them will alienate most prospects. Keep your terminology simple.

■ **RULE 50:** Ask open-ended questions to get prospects involved with you. For example, ask them how they feel about a subject. Questions that get a "yes" or "no" answer don't encourage conversation. You want your prospects to open up and talk to you. That's how you'll discover their needs and wants.

After your question produces a response, you can use the most powerful word in selling . . . "Why?" It will get you to their real feelings.

Chapter 27

CREDIBILITY — WHAT NOT TO DO

The initial seconds of an out-bound telemarketing call are the most crucial. Immediately identify yourself and the reason for your call.

It's easy to start a conversation by thanking pre-qualified leads for inquiring. This gives you a position of credibility because you are calling to provide something they want.

If you start out by asking prospects for a moment of their time, the implication is that you want something from them.

One of the worst approaches to a busy executive is beginning the call with, "How are you?" It suggests you have time for idle conversation. This can imply two things. You either are about to waste the executive's time with unnecessary chit-chat or you can't be very successful if you have extra time on your hands.

Stockbrokers who make hundreds of "dials" a day often start out their presentation by saying, "I know you're busy so I'll come straight to the point."

■ **RULE 51:** Be enthusiastic and assertive. It shows confidence and professionalism. Professionals demand to deal only with other professionals.

■ **RULE 52:** When an objection is raised, answer it immediately. Hesitation or delay can hurt your credibility.

Objections are a natural part of any interview, whether on the phone or in person. You'll have more success if you remember that objections actually indicate interest. Your prospects are inviting you to answer their concerns and make them feel comfortable.

■ **RULE 53:** Repeat what you and your prospect have agreed upon. Ask for the appointment or the sale. Always thank them and always hang up *last*.

■ **RULE 54:** When prospects call you, try not to put them on hold too long. According to *Inbound/Outbound Magazine*, seven out of ten callers to businesses are placed on hold. A third of those who hang up before you get on the line will never call back. However, if you provide a prerecorded message, music, or radio news during the "hold" time, about 85% will keep listening.

Chapter 28

FORBIDDEN PHRASES

KEY TERMS:

In-bound
Out-bound

During any phone call you or your staff may slip into the "forbidden zone" and use unfortunate phrases. Nancy Friedman suggests you recognize these phrases and eliminate them from your conversations:*

- *"I don't know."* This should be replaced with, *"Let me check and find out for you."*

- *"We can't do that."* Instead say, *" Let me see what I can do."*

- *"You'll have to..."* Callers don't have to do anything. There is a difference between ordering the caller to do something and saying, *"Here's how we can handle that. We suggest you ..."*

- *"Just a second."* This is a lie. It's a small one, but it can place the seed of doubt in the mind of your prospect through exaggeration. Use, *"It will take two or three minutes. Can you hold that long?"*

- *"No."* Saying no at the beginning of a sentence conveys total rejection to the prospect. By eliminating the word "no" from the start of sentences, you begin with a positive response.

■ **RULE 55:** Perhaps the most important and most overlooked aspect of **out-bound** or **in-bound** telemarketing is the simplest to cure. Too many people are too rude. Common courtesy should be your highest priority. Even if you don't make a sale, at least you've built some positive public relations by being courteous.

So be polite to your prospects. Don't interrupt or argue. Let them know you value what they have to say. And please don't have anything in your mouth (gum, cigarettes, *or foot*).

*Reprinted with permission of Nancy Friedman, The Telephone Doctor, a management consulting firm specializing in customer service and telephone skills. For further information call 1-800-882-9911 or write to: Box 777, Bridgeton, Missouri, 63044.

Part VI

DATABASE MARKETING

Creating A Greater Competitive Advantage

29. What Is A DataBase?
30. DataBase Information
31. How To Set Up and Use A DataBase

Chapter 29

WHAT IS A DATABASE?

KEY TERM:

Relationship Marketing

A DataBase is a computerized system of current information about customers and prospects. It allows you to mail very targeted, one-to-one promotions. That means you can send the right offer to the right people at the right time!

Computer power today allows you to improve your service to your clients and save time doing it. Supercomputers can process information today in 3 hours that took 7 days to complete just a couple of years ago. There are businesses today working with databases containing five million names on a personal computer.

According to the National Center of DataBase Marketing, the cost in 1973 to access a customer name, address, and purchase history was a little more than $7. Today, it's about a penny!

Alvin Toeffler, the futurist, said that knowledge and information are the currency of the future. In fact, it seems like we're at the dawning of a second industrial revolution: The Information Revolution. A predominant business activity today is collecting, processing, and using information.

Years ago, local merchants knew their customers intimately and catered to their individual preferences. This was called **relationship marketing**. The information was kept in each merchant's head. In many small communities relationship marketing still exists today as it did in the past.

Building relationships is at the heart of DataBase marketing. DataBase Marketing can work for any marketer today, whether you have 1,000 names or 100,000. By merging today's technology with the age-old concept of consumer information you can build a DataBase of your customers and prospects.

A DataBase of information is created for a company's own private use — not for others. It is a proprietary marketing weapon. Access is quick. There's no waiting for names from list companies. And you have more control of the information.

A DataBase allows you to analyze and market to specific segments of your list. For many years, direct marketers have known that up-to-date client information is the most reliable predictor of future purchase behavior. A current DataBase can help you analyze which clients to reach with your offer. This means you can pinpoint the best prospects for specific products. Your DataBase becomes an invaluable tool for pre-qualifying your prospects.

Chapter 30

DATABASE INFORMATION

A DataBase is only as good as the information in it. You should design, in advance, the reports you expect your DataBase to provide. Consider the following fields of information:

For Consumer DataBases
1. First name, last name (separate fields)
2. Street address, box or route number
3. City, state, zip+4, carrier route
4. Phone number (include area code)
5. Gender title (Mr/Ms)
6. Birthdate
7. Wealth rating (income/assets/home value)
8. Occupation

9. Interests (gardening, sports, travel, politics)
10. Source code (referred by relative, friend, professional)
11. Advertising medium (newspaper, direct mail, radio, seminars)

For Business Databases
1. Company name
2. Contact name (first, last)
3. Business title (VP Marketing)
4. Gender title (Mr/Ms)
5. Physical (street) address
6. Mailing address (P.O. Box)
7. City, state, zip+4, carrier route
8. Phone number (include area code)
9. Type of business
10. Sales volume
11. Number of employees

Why Use a DataBase? A DataBase is an amazing tool, but you must be willing to invest the time and money to establish it and keep it current. With continued increases in marketing costs, building a DataBase concentrates your resources where they will have the highest payoff. A DataBase also makes it more difficult for competitors to gain an advantage over you.

The benefits of an internal DataBase are:
1. Less expensive than repeated rental of outside lists.
2. Allows closer target marketing because of continuous enhancement with new information.
3. Provides instant access for quicker marketing decisions.
4. Offers more sophisticated testing and analysis of the file.

Create and develop your own DataBase if you:
1. Make repeated direct response promotions to the same prospects or clients.
2. Have trouble with minimum orders from list companies.
3. Are willing to invest $5,000 - $10,000 on your DataBase set-up (computer, printer, software, keypunch time).
4. Are willing to invest the time to learn how to operate the system. (Local community colleges or software suppliers are the best alternatives.)

Chapter 31

HOW TO SET UP AND USE A DATABASE

KEY TERMS:

Fields
Address Correction Requested

DataBases can be built from many different sources. One of the quickest ways to create a DataBase is to rent a list on computer diskette. Then supplement it with additional information you collect on your own.

If you rent lists, you probably want to go back to the list source at least once a year to get new names that have been added. About 20% of the general population moves each year. Businesses also move, and so do your contacts within businesses.

Once you have information, you need a computer software program with which to manage it. These programs place a picture of a document on the computer screen, not unlike a general information form on a piece of paper. The lines and spaces where you enter information are called **fields**. Many software programs you can buy off the shelf have pre-set fields. Some programs allow you to customize the fields as your information needs dictate.

If you're going to set up any special fields at all, try to think of every possible piece of information you might want to keep on each client or prospect. These might include elements I mentioned in Chapter 30, such as address, income, buying history, or anything else you might use for marketing purposes.

One of the best pieces of advice I've received is to read one of the monthly magazines on personal computers. You can learn a tremendous amount about computers and software this way. And it prepares you to ask better informed questions of suppliers.

When you mail first class, you automatically get a change of address notice if your prospect has moved. But if you use third class mail, you will not get the forwarding information back from the post office unless you print on the outside of the envelope or mailer the words, "**Address Correction Requested**." It is critical you use that line if you mail third class in order to keep your DataBase current and accurate.

Your DataBase will play a vital role in your marketing plan and business strategy. Because it is so important, you need to cultivate it with great care. That means continually updating it by adding new information and purging outdated information.

Part VII

LEAD MANAGEMENT

Controlling For Success

32. Testing
33. Balancing the Flow of Leads
34. When and Where To Mail
35. Inquiry Fulfillment

Chapter 32

TESTING

KEY TERMS:

Closure Rate
Rollout

It's amazing how often we guess what results will be, rather than getting facts from valid research and accurately projecting the outcome.

The answers to all your mailing questions should be based on test results, not intuition. Don't try to guess what your response rates will be. Compare the response and cost of every new test mailing with that of your standard mailing to know which is the most productive.

Your new offer of a "free analysis" may draw 10% more pre-qualified leads than your standard offer of "free information," but your **closure rate** (the portion of presentations converted to sales) may remain the same. It's easy to see that the new offer will make you more money just because you'll be talking to 10% more people.

■ **RULE 56:** When you test, test specifically, one thing at a time. Take one variable of your regular mailer and change it in a way you think will make it better. Test offers. Test lists. Test the look of your mailer. Test different timing. But test them separately — one at a time.

■ **RULE 57:** Test mailings usually consist of smaller quantities than regular mailings. You don't want to gamble large dollars on anything unproven. From results of tests you can project what your response rate should be when you mail a **rollout** or full mailing.

Chapter 33

BALANCING THE FLOW OF LEADS

The trick to having a steady flow of leads is to balance how many leads you need with how many you will get. If you manage a team of salespeople, or sell by yourself, you must first determine how many leads are needed per salesperson per week.

■ **RULE 58:** Once you have decided how many leads you want on a weekly basis, divide this quantity by your estimated response rate to determine how many promotions to mail.

For example, if you want 20 leads per week (4 per day) for each sales representative, divide 20 by your estimated response rate. If you expect a 2% response, 20 leads divided by .02 (2%) is 1,000. That's the number of mailers you need to send out on a weekly basis to get 20 leads for each salesperson.

As your quantity of needed leads changes or your response rate changes, you can revise your mailing volume appropriately. If your new test offer brings in a 3% return instead of 2%, you will only have to send out 667 mailers per week instead of 1,000. You'll notice very quickly that a slight change in response rate can make a large difference in the results of your mailing program.

■ **RULE 59:** Leads must be controlled when they are distributed to salespeople for initial follow up (either by phone or in person). Maintaining a consistent direct response program will help you avoid having too many or too few leads.

Sales people who get too many leads tend to prejudge them. The staff will start to guess which are the easiest sales. Tragically for your sales goals, this grading system is sometimes based on factors as simple as the prospect's handwriting.

The other side of balancing lead flow is having salespeople get too few leads. In this case they might not sell enough to cover their base salaries. The end result is often their departure from the firm, either voluntarily or not.

Chapter 34

WHEN AND WHERE TO MAIL

Mailing at the wrong time or to the wrong place can make your otherwise good promotion fall flat.

■ **RULE 60:** Timing is everything. You've heard that saying before. Well, in direct response marketing it is critically true.

Be careful before holidays. The idea is to have your mail arrive just *after* the holiday when people aren't thinking about their family visits, travel plans, or financial burdens.

The heaviest week for third class mail is between Christmas and New Year's Day for arrival just after the first of January. Be sensitive to all other holidays that call for family gatherings including the Fourth of July and Thanksgiving. Don't have your promotion mail when people are in the middle of a hectic schedule.

For business-to-business promotions, mail for arrival early in the week. You don't want your ideas to be forgotten over the weekend. Summer usually is a little slower because many people go on vacations and become difficult to contact.

Be aware of local happenings. A particular city might be hosting a celebration or sports event. An economic downturn could also affect your results. Other special times, like April 15th for income taxes and November 8th for elections need to be factored in.

Weather conditions can wreak havoc on your project. I once mailed a promotion into an area that experienced a devastating flood just as the mail was to be delivered. The results of the mailing, as you can imagine, were devastating also.

■ **RULE 61:** Where to mail is just as important as when. Mailing areas can be based on different considerations. For example, you may want prospects who live near your office or at least concentrated in one area so it's easy to see them in a short period of time.

Rural areas usually pull more response from consumers compared to city areas. In the city there is often more competition. In rural areas, people don't have someone around every corner trying to sell them something.

Most business-to-business promotions, however, don't have enough sales potential in small towns. There often aren't enough qualified prospects to make your direct response effort worthwhile. And even if there are, you still have to overcome the "buy local" prejudice.

Chapter 35

INQUIRY FULFILLMENT

It's important to work your leads when they are fresh. And make sure you are ready with a prepared follow-up package or have answers for expected questions you receive on the phone.

■ **RULE 62:** Respond to inquiries as quickly as possible while prospects still remember you and before they make a decision. If your follow-ups are too slow, your leads may become someone else's customers. But remember, older pre-qualified leads are always better than cold prospects.

I usually try to have the elements of the inquiry fulfillment package ready just after the mail drops. A general letter can be worded so that any salesperson can sign it. Make sure you have enough brochures on hand for your expected response. I'd suggest printing a few extra. Better to have too many than not enough.

■ **RULE 63:** In order for your sales force to do the best job possible, they must understand the complete lead generation campaign. Support your sales staff by providing this information:

- Samples of the mailers and follow-up materials prospects will receive
- A description of the list(s) used
- Details on timing of the program
- Sample questions to expect

Many managers dole out information about programs on a poorly devised "need to know" basis. Your sales people and your telemarketers must understand the goals of each program and what information you want your prospects to be given when they respond.

Imagine your sales force, armed with inadequate information, selling different benefits for the same product. If you've determined that your product's major benefit is quality, you don't want your sales people beating the drum for price, do you? This can only lead to less than expected sales.

Part VIII

LEAD GENERATION BUSINESS STRATEGIES

Ideas for Building a Better Business

36. Six Hard Knocks Strategies
      Persistence
      List Deliverability
      Testing
      Action
      Client Information
      Prepare for Success
37. Does Lead Generation Pay?

Chapter 36

SIX HARD-KNOCKS STRATEGIES

Six strategies have proven over the years to be cornerstones of success. Blend these business ideas into your development of lead generation programs.

Persistence.

You can't sell everyone. Your best prospects may be perfectly happy with their current product, service, price, or salesperson.

Many people feel obligated to buy from relatives or to reciprocate buying from their own customers. And loyalty does exist, even for less-than-perfect products and service, because people are resistant to change.

If no problem or dissatisfaction exists in the mind of your prospects, or if they're obligated to their source, they have no significant reason to switch to you.

■ **RULE 64:** If you can't improve your leads' situations, don't badger them about it. Just keep in touch with them periodically (I recommend quarterly for most businesses) with a letter, phone call, information package, or newsletter. The day will come when their situation will change and they'll appreciate your professionalism, consideration, and persistence.

List Deliverability.

You'll discover that in every project a portion of your list is undeliverable or non-contactable. It's a normal occurrence, so don't be overly concerned.

Most list rental companies continually update their lists, and you'll do the same for your DataBase. But people and businesses move or die every day, so some of every list fails to reach its destination.

In the mass compiled list business, 90% deliverability is considered acceptable. I've listened to business people complain about 50 incorrect names out of 5,000 (a 1% error factor). I've also heard people gripe when one individual name was missing from a list.

■ **RULE 65:** Concentrate on that vast majority of your list which is good. It should make you plenty of money. Don't worry if a small portion is undeliverable.

Testing.

■ **RULE 66:** Test your promotional ideas. What works is what counts. Find what works and make that your standard. Then continue testing different ideas against that standard to find what works better. What works today may not work tomorrow. If you don't test new ideas, you'll eventually mail an unproductive promotion.

Action.

■ **RULE 67:** More is lost through inaction than improper action. Start planning and executing your lead generation program right now. Aggressive action gets results. Don't wait for everything to be perfect.

Client Information.

Many companies and sales people keep a file of detailed information on their customers. It's how they know when to send birthday greetings or congratulations on special events like a client's *alma mater* winning a ball game. Chances are you keep such a file. It might be on a computer disk or in your head.

■ **RULE 68:** However you gather information and wherever you keep it, the most important thing to do is use it! Collecting information and not using it is like buying a car and never driving it. If you're not going to use it, why waste your time and money?

Prepare for Success.

■ **RULE 69:** One of the worst things that can happen is to be so successful with a mailing that you can't respond to your pre-qualified leads in a timely manner. In this case you've probably been caught flatfooted and unprepared to take advantage of your own success.

Often this is due to underestimating the response rate. Whatever the reason, if it happens, you must forge ahead.

Even if your follow-up package does not include a personalized letter and beautiful brochure, get the requested information to the prospect as soon as possible. Remember that a good-looking piece is nice, but not crucial.

Hire temporary staff if necessary to help insure inquires are answered promptly. Keep your eye out for the best of the temporaries. You'll probably have to hire them full time to handle the flood of business from your lead generation programs.

Chapter 37

DOES LEAD GENERATION PAY?

You need to make a profit on every lead generating promotion. If you can't, something needs to change. Maybe the mailer cost is too high. Maybe you need a new prospect list. Maybe you need to work on techniques to close more sales per inquiry.

■ **RULE 70:** Always predict your success or failure in terms of profit or loss before going ahead with a direct response lead generation program.

Look at the examples on the next page to see how lead generation can pay off. Then estimate your own income using projected response, average sales, and your own closure rates and commissions.

WORKSHEET

	Insurance	Real Estate	Financial Planning	Your Business
Number of Mailers:	5,000	1,000	1,000	_____
Response Rate: (Responses divided by quantity mailed)	2%	1/2%	1%	_____
Number of Pre-Qualified Leads: (Mailers x response rate)	100	5	10	_____
Closure Rate: (Number of sales divided by sales presentations)	25%	20%	50%	_____
Number of Sales: (Closure rate x leads)	25	1	5	_____
Average Sale:	$800	$150,000	$10,000	_____
Total Sales Dollars:	$20,000	$150,000	$50,000	_____
Commission Rate:	40%	3%	10%	_____
Total Commission:	$8,000	$4,500	$5,000	_____
Less Mailing Investment: (Lists, printing, and postage)	($1,500)	($300)	($300)	_____
Net Income: (Commission less investment)	$6,500	$4,200	$4,700	_____

Conclusion

We began our journey into direct response lead generation by looking at people — the people who have responded to your direct response efforts. You'll remember I called them "pre-qualified leads."

In our final chapters, we looked at pre-qualified leads again, but this time they were part of your DataBase — your list of people who are most likely to buy your products.

Through our journey I've tried to explain to you how to avoid the mistakes I've either made or seen other people make. I've tried to give you painlessly what has taken me tens of thousands of hours to learn. My teacher has been experience. Hopefully, as *your* teacher, I have been able to give you the best of my experience.

Now that you know how to do it, keep in mind that learning by doing is the best way to find what works to produce pre-qualified leads. And testing to improve on what works is the best way for you to increase your success.

Reading this book may well take the place of years of trial and error for you. It will probably save you thousands of dollars. If it doesn't make you more sales — more profit — faster, then something's wrong.

If you run into a problem executing any of the steps I've given you, please call me. I want to know because I want you to succeed like I have.

Thank you for reading my book!

Allyn Kramer

Listing of Rules

■ **RULE 1:**   The best way to get new sales people started is to get them in front of a pre-qualified lead.

■ **RULE 2:**   Target marketing to generate pre-qualified leads begins with two basic steps: 1) determine what specific product or service you want to promote; and 2) decide who is your most likely prospect for it.

■ **RULE 3:**   Construct a customer profile of the type of person most likely to buy each of your products. Paint a word picture of that person.

■ **RULE 4:**   Demographics tell you if the market you've targeted is able to buy your product. Demographics give you the quantitative information about prospects in your market such as where they live, how much income they earn and how old they are.

■ **RULE 5:**   Psychographics tell you if your market wants to buy your product. Psychographics give you the qualitative information about your market such as how they buy and why they buy.

■ **RULE 6:**   Synchrographics tell you if the market is ready to buy your product. Synchrographics give you the time when something is going to affect your market such as a birth, marriage, sale of a house or business, or retirement.

■ **RULE 7:**   Targeting a group that is knowledgeable about your product category costs you less and takes less time and money than marketing to a group you have to educate.

■ **RULE 8:** Advertising (like most newspaper and magazine ads) that promotes your company's image will never pull immediate responses. It's not designed to do that. A promotion that pin-points to your reader exactly what your product benefits are and tells them how and when to respond will produce immediate responses.

■ **RULE 9:** To generate fewer leads with more quality:

- Tell the price of your product or service that you're selling.
- Tell your prospects that a salesperson will call when they respond.
- Make them pay their own postage. This requires more commitment and means they're really interested.
- Ask qualifying questions such as phone numbers, work address, or financial information.

■ **RULE 10:** To generate more leads with less quality.

- Give free gifts or offer a substantial price discount.
- Make it easy for the leads to respond with a toll-free phone number or postage paid reply envelope.
- If sales calls are not part of the follow-up, say so. The person responding will have less fear of getting a high pressure sales pitch.
- Tell prospects only enough to make them curious. Curiosity alone should get prospects to say "Tell me more."

■ **RULE 11:** When you're thinking about renting a list, ask about the original source of the list.

■ **RULE 12:** Ask how often new names are added to the list, not how often it is updated. An update can be as simple as adding a few phone numbers. A new compilation on the other hand, means that new names have been added.

■ **RULE 13:** 20% of the general population relocates every year. Businesses move and die just like people. You need to recognize that no list is perfect. Even if you compile your own list today, tomorrow it will probably be out of date.

■ **RULE 14:** Find out if telephone follow-up lists are available. Some lists have names and addresses only. Some have phone numbers for just a portion of the names. Some have phone numbers for all the names. Don't assume anything. Ask before you rent a list.

■ **RULE 15:** Eliminate or purge your current customers from your lead generation program. This not only saves you postage money, but it also keeps you from looking unprofessional to your customers.

■ **RULE 16:** Postage often accounts for 20% to 50% of the cost of your direct mail promotion. The question about postage that most mailers ask is, "Can you be just as effective using third class mail versus first class mail?" The answer is "Maybe."

■ **RULE 17:** Carrier route sorting can save you a considerable amount of money because you're doing some of the Post Office's work. The amount saved may well be enough to cover the cost of renting the list.

■ **RULE 18:** Don't overlook or reject the idea of addressing your mailing to "Occupant" or "Resident". It can be beneficial in certain circumstances.

■ **RULE 19:**   Since most lead generation packages try to target prospects more specifically than everyone on the block, you can waste money renting an "Occupant" list. Without a personal name it also has the immediate perception of "junk" mail and may promptly be thrown away.

■ **RULE 20:**   The more information your prospects are given, the easier it is for them to make a decision regarding your offer.

■ **RULE 21:**   With few exceptions, you will see that an offer with something "Free" will generate more responses than the same offer with nothing "Free."

■ **RULE 22:**   The word "new" is one that always gets people's attention. The American public is constantly taught by the fashion industry to want the very latest, whatever that may be.

■ **RULE 23:**   Anything given away must be analyzed for its impact on cost per lead and cost per sale.

■ **RULE 24:**   Giving away something related to your product or service will generate responses from people who are interested in what you are selling. If the give-away is linked to your product or service, you should have fewer problems with "freebie junkies".

■ **RULE 25:**   Testimonials and case histories lend credibility to your offer. If you want to use these, don't rely on just one. The secret to using them successfully is to bombard your readers with as many testimonials as possible.

■ **RULE 26:** Write the way you talk. The average working American reads at the 8th grade level. Use short words, short sentences and short paragraphs.

■ **RULE 27:** Be specific (such as "70 Rules"). Be immediate (such as "Call right now for free information"). People like numbers and they don't like to wait.

■ **RULE 28:** To be successful, humor must touch virtually every reader. By targeting a specific group you have a better chance of succeeding with humor than addressing a general audience.

■ **RULE 29:** When you write, look for action verbs.

■ **RULE 30:** Contractions help your readers hear your words as though they were being spoken.

■ **RULE 31:** The word YOU is almost as magic as FREE and NEW. Use it again and again. It creates a one-to-one relationship between you and your reader.

■ **RULE 32:** The outside envelope, brochure headline, the inside address, signature line, and P.S. are HOT SPOTS. They're the first places people look.

■ **RULE 33:** How large can your headline be? It can be very large. In fact, it can take up to a third of the ad space or brochure panel.

■ **RULE 34:** There are six different kinds of headlines:

1. Commanding
2. How-to
3. Question
4. News

5. Testimonial
6. Intrigue

RULE 35: Because of today's mail box glut, your promotion needs to stand out in the stack of mail. Half the battle in direct mail is to get your piece opened.

RULE 36: What works today will eventually lose its punch. For your mailings to continue to be productive, you must continue to test new ideas against your standard mailer.

RULE 37: Concentrate on using the right list and promoting the right offer. The look of the mailer is secondary.

RULE 38: Give your prospects different opportunities to respond favorably.

RULE 39: You'll get the quickest responses by offering a phone number to call. The prospects who call are the best leads since they want to talk now, not sometime after they mail in the reply card and you get around to answering it.

RULE 40: Remember to include a project code so you can keep track of how many responses you get from each mailing. This can be as simple as a letter or number unique to each mailing. You can place this project code on the reply card or label.

RULE 41: Remember these key points in your follow-up letter: Spelling, Thank you, Information, Friends.

RULE 42: If you decide to hire an ad agency, be certain it employs experts in direct response marketing.

■ **RULE 43:**   The easiest way to approach telemarketing is with a follow-up to your pre-qualified direct mail inquiries.

■ **RULE 44:**   There's a right time and a wrong time to call.

- Consumer prospects should be called in the evenings (after dinner time) and on weekends.
- Senior citizen retirees are best reached in morning rather than in the evening.
- Business owners and managers can often be reached directly before or after regular business hours or on Saturday mornings when no one is in the office to screen their calls.

■ **RULE 45:**   Work from a prepared outline, not a script. Few people can sound spontaneous and believable while reading a script. An outline gives you the information you need and still lets you sound natural.

■ **RULE 46:**   Always smile into the phone. As odd as it sounds, your smile will carry over into your voice. Prospects will perceive you as friendlier.

■ **RULE 47:**   Stick to one idea and be brief. As soon as you start bringing in unnecessary details, you're sunk, especially with busy executives.

■ **RULE 48:**   Use the prospect's name throughout your conversation. It invites friendliness.

■ **RULE 49:**   Since most people don't understand technical terms, using them will alienate most prospects, so keep your terminology simple.

■ **RULE 50:**   Ask open-ended questions to get prospects involved with you. Questions that get a "yes" or "no" answer don't encourage your prospects to open-up. Use the most powerful word in selling: "Why?" It will get you to their real feelings.

■ **RULE 51:**   Be enthusiastic and assertive. It shows confidence and professionalism. Professionals demand to deal only with other professionals.

■ **RULE 52:**   When an objection is raised, answer it immediately. Hesitation or delay can hurt your credibility.

■ **RULE 53:**   Repeat what you and your prospect have agreed upon. Ask for the appointment or the sale. Always thank them and always hang up *last*.

■ **RULE 54:**   Provide a pre-recorded message or music if your prospects must be put on hold.

■ **RULE 55:**   Common courtesy should be your highest priority with out-bound or in-bound telemarketing.

■ **RULE 56:**   When you test, test specifically, one thing at a time. Take one variable of your regular mailer and change it in a way you think will make it better.

■ **RULE 57:**   Test mailings usually consist of smaller quantities than regular mailings. You don't want to gamble large dollars on anything unproven. From results of tests you can project what your response rate should be when you mail a rollout or full mailing.

■ **RULE 58:**   Once you have decided how many leads you want on a weekly basis, divide this quantity by your estimated response rate to determine how many promotions to mail.

■ **RULE 59:**   Leads must be controlled when they are distributed to salespeople for initial follow-up (either by phone or in person). Maintaining a consistent direct response program will help you avoid having too many or too few leads.

■ **RULE 60:**   Timing is everything. You've heard that saying before. Well, in direct response marketing it is critically true.

■ **RULE 61:**   Where to mail is just as important as when. Mailing areas can be based on different considerations. For example, you may want prospects who live near your office or at least concentrated in one area so it's easy to see them in a short period of time.

■ **RULE 62:**   Respond to inquiries as quickly as possible while prospects still remember you and before they make a decision. If your follow-ups are too slow, your leads may become someone else's customers. But remember, older pre-qualified leads are always better than cold prospects.

■ **RULE 63:**   In order for your sales force to do the best job possible, they must understand the complete lead generation campaign. Support your sales staff by providing this information:

- Samples of the mailers and follow-up materials prospects will receive
- A description of the list(s) used
- Details on timing of the program
- Sample questions to expect

■ **RULE 64:**   If you can't improve your leads' situations, don't badger them about it. Just keep in touch with them periodically (I recommend quarterly for most businesses) with a letter, phone call, information package, or newsletter. The day will come when their situation will change and they'll appreciate your professionalism, consideration and persistence.

■ **RULE 65:** Concentrate on that vast majority of your list which is good. It should make you plenty of money. Don't worry if a small portion is undeliverable.

■ **RULE 66:** Test your promotional ideas. What works is what counts. Find what works and make that your standard. Then continue testing different ideas against that standard to find what works better. What works today may not work tomorrow. If you don't test your ideas, you'll eventually mail an unproductive promotion.

■ **RULE 67:** More is lost through inaction than improper action. Start planning and executing your lead generation program right now. Aggressive action gets results. Don't wait for everything to be perfect.

■ **RULE 68:** However you gather information and wherever you keep it, the most important thing to do is use it! Collecting information and not using it is like buying a car and never driving it. If you're not going to use it, why waste your time and money?

■ **RULE 69:** One of the worst things that can happen is to be so successful with a mailing that you can't respond to your pre-qualified leads in a timely manner. In these cases you've probably been caught flat-footed and unprepared to take advantage of your own success.

■ **RULE 70:** Always predict your success or failure in terms of profit or loss before going ahead with a direct response lead generation program.

Glossary of Additional Terms

Card Deck: Type of co-op mailing which includes a number of reply post cards enclosed in a single outer wrapper (often cellophane).

Co-Op Mailing: Shared mailing with a number of different offers inserted into a single envelope or package. Cost of postage is dramatically reduced for each promotional piece. Ususally the response rate is reduced also, compared to unique individual mailings.

Cross Section: A random selection of names from a list which is representative of the entire list. Used for testing purposes to determine if all names are worth using. Also known as an "Nth" selection.

Cheshire Labels: Names and addresses printed on plain white computer paper without glue or gum backing. Addresses are usually four across and eleven down on a page. These labels *must* be applied to the mailing piece by a professional mail service with automated equipment.

Decoy: A unique name and address included in a list and used to insure a mailing sample is returned to the mailer or list provider. The decoy name will determine any unauthorized list usage or track delivery time. Also known as a "dummy" or "seed" name.

Galley Listing: A computer printout of information, such as a phone list. Also known as a manuscript.

Key Code: Same as Project Code. Used to track mailing results. Also known as a "Source Code" or "Mail Code".

Lettershop: A business that assembles and prepares promotions for mailing.

Multi-Family Dwelling Unit (MFDU): Addresses represented by apartment or condominium dwellers only.

National Change of Address (NCOA): A list of recent movers from change of address notifications received by the Post Office. Can be used as a list selection or information to enhance a house file.

Nixie: An undeliverable address.

Pressure Sensitive Lables: "Peel 'n stick" labels which can be pulled off and hand affixed to a mailing piece.

Sectional Center Facility (SCF): A processing facility of the U.S. Postal Service represented by the first three digits of a five digit zip code. Used in list selection for convenience. To select all zip codes in a large city, it is easier to request only the SCF (all zip codes beginning with the same first three digits). For example, all 49 zips in the city of Dallas, Texas can be pulled by using one selection of the SCF 752.

Self-Mailer: A promotional piece that mails without an envelope, such as a folded three panel mailer with a perforated reply card.

Single Family Dwelling Unit (SFDU): An individual home address. Used for list selection to eliminate apartment dwellers.

Standard Industrial Classification (SIC): Categories of businesses as established by the U.S. Department of Commerce. Useful in selection or omission of specific types of businesses when ordering a list.

Title: Personal identification (such as Mr., Ms, or Dr.) or business function identification (such as Purchasing Director or Marketing VP).

White Paper: A response which can not be tracked to a specific promotion because no project code is available.

Index

40-40-20 Rule   98

A

Action verbs   79
Acquisition cost   17
Ad agencies
    working with   108
Address Correction Requested   125
Advertising
    and ad agencies   108
    and direct response   29
    and image   65, 107
    tracking   21
Attention
    getting   95
    holding   50

B

Benefits   65

C

Call-to-action   28
Carrier route sorting   44
Case histories   70
Clip art   106
Closure rate   128
Cold calls   21
Compiled lists   36
Contractions   80
Copy (text)   71
Cost per lead   60
Cost per sale   60

Credibility   114
Customer lists   37

D

DataBase   119
    fields   125
Deliverability of lists   137
Demographics   23
Desire   50
Direct mail   30
    and newspapers   30
Door-to-door sales   21

E

Envelopes
    and attention   86
    and testing   101
    postage paid   33
    types   95

F

Features   65
Fields   125
Follow-up
    and leads   133
    and timing   133
    materials   134
Follow-up letter   104
Forbidden phrases   116
Free
    use of   58, 63
Freebie junkies   63

G

Generic
  messages 28

H

Headlines 88
Hot Spots 86
Humor 74

I

Interest 50
Involvement device 53

L

Leads
  cost of 59
  hard 55
  managing 129
  soft 54
Letter
  follow-up 104
Lists
  broker 39
  compiled 36
  customer 37
  deliverability 137
  manager 38
  owner 38
  response 36

M

Magic words 56
Mailer types 95
Marketing
  targeted 22
  mass audience 28
  traditional 26
Merge-purge 42

N

Names 19
New
  use of 58
Newsletters 95

O

Occupant mail 45
Offer
  and credibility 70
  building-in desire 50
  general 31, 49
  "let's get acquainted" 42
  time-sensitive 44

P

Package 30
Positioning
  physical 82
  viewpoint 84
Post office 45
Postage
  saving money on 42, 43, 45
Pre-qualified lead
  generation 17
Pre-qualified leads 19
Project code 101 *See also* Tracking
Promotion
  hard 54
  soft 54
Prospecting 20, 21
Prospects 18
  and direct marketing 21
Psychographics 23
Purge 42

Q

Questions
  objections to   115
  open-ended   113
  wrong   114

R

Relationship marketing   120
Reply card   30, 53
Response
  and ad agencies   108
  and ease of use   50
  and phone calls   101
  and project codes   101
  and quantity   33
  and the word "no"   117
Response device   99, 101
Response lists   36
Response rate   31
Rollout   128

S

Sale
  cost of   59
Sales staff support   134
Setup and punch   75
Spelling   105
Synchrographics   23

T

Target marketing   22, 24
Telemarketing
  and cold calls   110
  and forbidden phrases   116-117
  and receptionists   111
  as a follow up   110
  in-bound   117
  out-bound   117
  to business owners   111
  to consumers   111
  to seniors   111
  when to   111

Testimonials   70
Testing   127-128
Third class mail   44
  and saving money   43
  vs. first class   44
Timing mail delivery   131
Tracking   21
Traditional marketing   26

U

Update   39
Understanding   50

V

Viewpoint Positioning   84

W

Words
  action   79
  boring   79
Worksheet   141

Z

Zip code sequencing   44

An Invitation

Whenever you discover you want help or advice about any aspect of pre-qualified lead generation, you can call us. Whether it's business or consumer lists, or complete direct mail programs, we're available to share our experience with you. Please contact us at:

KRAMER LEAD MARKETING GROUP
11884 Greenville Avenue, Suite 106 • Dallas, Texas 75243

972-644-6000   800-447-0533

To Order Additional Copies of
HOW TO MASTER THE ART OF LEAD GENERATION
mail this coupon with payment of $12.95
plus $3.00 (shipping and handling) to:

Prestonwood Press
P.O. Box 795892
Dallas, Texas 75379

Name _____
Title _____
Company _____
Address _____
City/State/Zip _____
Phone (_____)_____